The Killing Closet
A Memoir

V.L. Brunskill

Published by:
Southern Yellow Pine (SYP) Publishing
4351 Natural Bridge Rd.
Tallahassee, FL 32305

www.syppublishing.com

The contents and opinions expressed in this book do not necessarily reflect the views and opinions of Southern Yellow Pine Publishing, nor does the mention of brands or trade names constitute endorsement.

ISBN-13: 978-1-59616-130-6
ISBN-13: ePub 978-1-59616-131-3
ISBN-13: Kindle 978-1-59616-132-0

Library of Congress Control Number: 2023946786

Interior photos courtesy of V.L. Brunskill
Front Cover Design: Kimberly Randall

Praise for *The Killing Closet*

"I'm astounded by the bravery it took to tell this story. *The Killing Closet* is not for the faint of heart. But heart is the key word. This memoir is terrifying to read as Brunskill lays out still-fresh brutality, but at the same time, balances the darkness with a clear and defined sense of redemption. To find understanding, and even hope, inside a landscape filled with monsters is no easy feat. But it's worth the read to understand the heart of a survivor. This book will make you want to hold the hand of someone you love and never let go."

—Brian Panowich, International Best-Selling Author of *Bull Mountain* and *Nothing But The Bones*

"A soul searing story of abuse that pits survival versus untethered evil."

—Jackie K Cooper, author of *The Wisdom of Winter, Memory's Mist, Journey of a Gentle Southern Man*

"*The Killing Closet* is at once a hard-hitting exploration of a childhood lost to violence and a keen-edged narrative about the dual nature of loving and hating.

—Karen Salyer McElmurray, author of *Voice Lessons, Wanting Radiance, Surrendered Child*

"*The Killing Closet*, is without a doubt one of the more riveting (and oft chilling) accounts I've ever read. Time after time, I found myself asking how Brunskill and her family lived through what she describes. I found myself in tears, or angered on her behalf, and horrified by her experiences. Finally, came my admiration for her nuanced handling of what, ultimately, is delicate subject matter indeed, and I'm sure that, like me, none of her readers will be able to put this breath-taking book down before it's end."

—**Rosemary Daniell, award-winning author of *Fatal Flowers: On Sin, Sex and Suicide in the Deep South* and nine other books of poetry and prose**

The Killing Closet

A Memoir

Epigraph

I thought I'd been writing ['The Great Santini'] 'cause I hated my father, and what stunned me when I came to the last line was that I was writing the book because I loved my father and had spent my whole life trying to find something to love in him.

Pat Conroy

I forgive you of all your past transgressions. Be free of them and live here in peace.

Elijah Van Dah-Gotham (Fox Television)

Hide nothing, for time, which sees all and hears all, exposes all.

Sophocles

TRIGGER WARNING

This book deals with domestic abuse, child abuse, animal abuse, adoption, and gender topics. While the author has taken great lengths to ensure the subject matter is dealt with in a compassionate and respectful manner, it may be troubling for some readers. Discretion is advised.

Table of Contents

Prologue

I wait for him among the long wool overcoats and rain boots of the cramped hall closet. Unzipping the leather case, I caress the trigger of Dad's beloved weapon, the metal cold against my pointer finger. I hold the shell in my hand for a moment before copying my father's exactness to load the weapon. The click of the chamber, once a terrifying foreshadowing, thrills me. There is power in knowing that I will take my father's life when he returns from work.

Shuffling from the closet, I lean around the corner to aim at the open front door. The cement stoop, visible through the screen insert in the storm door, cools in the shade of dusk. Despair combined with the stuffy scent of rarely used items makes it hard to breathe. Living in fear for so long has frayed my options to one. My heart jumps when I hear Dad's truck in the driveway. I look up at the marble crucifix. Porcelain Jesus stares back. Perspiration trickles down my back. I lick my lips at the idea of freedom.

Kneeling at attention, I rest the butt of the weapon on the wood floor, wondering what is keeping my father from his fate. Gazing at the cross, I think that Dad's loathing makes me love the holy man more. Realistically rendered, the tiny being wears a pained expression. His bloodied hands and feet seem to pulsate with hurt, and then he appears to nod. The shock forces me to sit back on my heels. *What else can I do?* I ask the figure, hugging the gun to my chest.

Whether hallucination or miracle, the vision startles me into retreat. Hurt your father, hurt yourself is his message; I can't say it is an actual thought. It feels more like a gush of wind invading every pore, an exhale so big it knocks me back, making my eyes water. Removing my finger from the trigger, the flame of vengeance drains. Crawling back into the closet, I cover my mouth to silence my cavernous breathing, sliding the door shut just in time. Dad's big steps pass in the hall.

"Where the fuck is everyone?" he yells, and we begin again.

PART I—BEFORE ME

1 From the Ashes

I was eleven years old when I failed to kill my father. Like a throat tickle that no amount of water might ease, the need for his demise was my constant childhood companion. Kitchen cutlery, garden implements, and my baby brother's baseball bat were the weapons of my imagination. An arsenal of possibilities.

What kind of person wishes for their father's death? I ask myself this question a lot. Was I evil or simply unable to process any other means of escape? Even the most desperate circumstances do not usually lead children to plot, pray, and scheme a parental murder. Perhaps, planning my father's death was easy due to a survival chemistry wired in my infant brain by the unplanned circumstance of my birth.

I was not Joe Selbach's daughter by conception. I was born outside his genetic brood, arriving in New York City along with the Beatles. Two American invasions, one fan-fared, the other dreaded. No father figure existed in my first moments. Although, the first father might have been there in the first mother's mind as she writhed in labor. A replaying of his small frame dressed in army green fatigues and his angry reaction to her pregnancy. The way he threatened to punch her pregnant belly, turning at the last moment to pummel his red Nova instead.

In the physical realm of that sanitized public hospital bed, where hundreds of poverty-laden women had pushed forth their babies, thoughts of the sperm donor lingered and disappeared. My fair-skinned first mother clung to me, whispering assurances that we would be okay. She was young, unmarried, and an immigrant from the smallest town in the farthest Province of Canada.

Did I believe her assurances when she said goodbye within hours of my first breath? "You'll be okay. You'll have a great family. I love you." Or were they the pain-driven mutterings of a mother trying to convince herself? For each day she awoke with me growing inside her was another day of hiding me under a girdle and loose garments so that her boss at the Five and Dime would not notice. She was unmarried, alone, frightened, and convinced by a misguided adoption system that giving me away was better than social suicide.

I was removed from her belly's soft, warm swell on Christmas Eve, 1964. In that swift ripping, my first mother and I became as alone as two humans can be.

After my relinquishment is a blank space of seven secret months spent in four foster homes. Only the ghostly bottle-feeders know who they are. The records are gone, tossed from my reality along with those formative months. I do not know where I was or who cared for me during these blank times. My singular hint is a single black-and-white photograph. It is the one image of me before I began my Selbach saga. Distrust and bewilderment define my infant expression as I lay in a pram too large for my premature size. The edge of the photograph is cut off, perhaps to protect a foster parent's identity.

The first father was also a killer. Special Forces. Lifetime soldier. So perhaps he donated more than fertilization for my life, casting my ability to plan my adoptive father's demise.

~ ~ ~

The couple who would become my adoptive parents met at a long-since demolished roller rink, near what was once the Corona Ash Dump. The Valley of Ashes was no longer a 1920s dumping ground for New York City's ash waste. In its place stood Flushing Meadows Corona Park. It was 1961, and the vast park bustled with hardworking men preparing the 646-acre expanse of land for the 1964 World's Fair.

Lillian Barbiera's first memory of meeting Joe Selbach is the tremor of sound surrounding her first look at him. That he arrived with booming accompaniment is no surprise.

Song and chatter climaxed and waxed with waves of pulsating overhead lights, making Lillian feel dizzy and delighted. At almost nineteen, she was in that prime of womanhood when skin is taut and curves have yet to plump in the middle. Tomboyish and naïve, she kept pace with the daredevil dancers who showed off that Saturday night. Risking bruises and breaks while falling headfirst into a life of them, she skated to impress Joe, who worked behind the graffiti-covered skate rental stand, polishing a skate wheel and looking bored. She stared at him until he looked up fixing his piercing blue eyes on her like prey. Instead of smiling at her flirtation, he appeared to sneer.

Lillian watched from the back wall of the rink, shifting her weight from leg to leg, hoping for the ache in her ankles to subside. When she realized that Joe was looking her way, she pushed past the pain to circle the rink again. Tucking her blouse into her ankle-length skirt, she touched the toe pad of her skate to the floor to stop near him but instead slammed full force into the metal railing.

Joe looked back, wearing the intense look of a hunter. Six years older than Lillian, he wore his dark blond hair in a neat side part, slicked down with a touch of Brylcreem. His teeth bright and straight, he stood wide-legged, his chest forward. He nodded a militaristic, matter-of-fact nod.

Wanting to look cute, Lillian turned away to suck in the corners of her mouth, creating a kewpie doll pout. But when she looked back, Joe was gone. Destiny escorted her from the rail to the rink-side bench, where she waved at her neighborhood friend Bella. Pointing at her feet, she let Bella know she would be over as soon as she took off her skates.

Bella waved back, lifting a soggy French fry in the air, and Lillian joined her after removing her skates.

Joe strutted up to the women's table, a pale, Germanic giant in the sea of mostly Puerto Rican, Italian, and Negro patrons. Joe's deep voice rose atop the bass of the circus-like music. He sounded sexy and experienced when he introduced himself, "Hey, Hayadooin? I'm Joe. Dem ankles holding up?"

"What's it to ya?" Lillian crossed her shapely legs. It was an Ingrid Bergman pose she'd practiced. "God, he's a looker," she whispered to Bella.

The burst of screeching giggles that followed turned Joe's grin into a tight-lipped mope. His hands drew into fists. "What's so funny?" he asked.

Lillian replied in a whipped cream purr. "Nothing. Uh, wanna join us?" She pointed to an empty chair.

"Sure," Joe agreed, unclenching his hands. He rotated the chair, straddling the seat, "Break's over soon. Just got a few minutes."

"How long you been working here?" Lillian asked, leaning her chin on her hand and resting her elbow on the table. The music in the rink slowed to a whining waltz, thick with calliope and short on melody.

Joe spoke louder, "Two weeks. Side job." He looked around the lobby, making sure his boss was still out of earshot.

"What's your other job?" Lillian chomped on the bait. Sipping the last of her vanilla egg creme, she dangled the paper straw seductively between her full lips.

4

Joe cocked his head and clucked, "State Trooper. On furlough. Just working at dis dump for extra cash."

"Really?" Lillian stretched her neck, nervous and intrigued. "Cops are fab."

"If you like the buzz cut type," Bella chimed.

Bella put a hand over her mouth to block Joe's view, saying, "This one's got all the earmarks of a fugazi. Don't go."

"Come on, Bella, he's no fugazi. What's fake? Looks real to me, and he's gorgeous," Lillian whispered back.

Joe leaned close to Lillian's ear, "Wanna go outside? It'll be quieter."

She beamed. She pointed toward the entrance with tingling cheeks and a barely veiled blush. "Be right back." They passed the line of thirsty skater couples waiting at the snack bar. Lillian matched Joe's brisk pace, savoring the attention they garnered as he pushed his way through the crowd.

Crisp air and shadows cast by several spotlights welcomed them into the parking lot. A line of muscle cars cramped the walkway. They faced each other, standing in an empty parking space, each considering the romantic possibilities.

"Nice night." Lillian looked up, shading her eyes from the harsh light. "Can't see the stars, though."

"Yeah," Joe joined her skyward glance. "City has that effect on things, makes 'em disappear." Clearing his throat awkwardly, he asked, "You skating tomorrow? I get an hour for lunch if you wanna meet." His tone coaxed and bullied simultaneously, hinting at a need for caution that Lillian ignored.

"Can't tomorrow. I'm Catholic. Church," she said, looking down at the cracked pavement where a small weed grew despite daily stomping. "Not super religious," she defended. "Just Dad. If I don't go, he'll blow a gasket." She rubbed her damaged knuckles, a punishment delivered by the Mother Superior when she and her Catechism classmates giggled at the idea of virgin birth during class.

"Ditch it anyway." Joe snorted, "Religion's for patsies."

The sound of a passing ambulance squealed from nearby Van Wyck Expressway. Lillian increased her volume to compensate for the racket, "Nah. My parents are strict. All us kids gotta go. As long as we live under their roof, you know." She bit her lip.

"What about after?" Joe stuffed his hand in the pocket of his pegged pants, kicking at a cigarette butt.

The wind blew a newspaper across the pavement towards them. Lillian stepped back. The paper clung to the metal lamp post. "Well, we're Sicilian. Sunday's a family thing, spaghetti and all. We ain't crooks, though," she defended. "Name's Lillian Barbiera."

"Yeah? Well, how's a guy supposed to get a date with a wop, then?" he winked. "I worked with a few guineas. Hard workers."

The low groan of engine noise interrupted the conversation as a TWA jet rumbled from Idlewild Airport. They looked up, watching the jetliner disappear.

"Pick any day but Sunday, I guess," Lillian answered. "And we don't like that word, wop. You know what it means?"

Joe shook his head.

"My uncle said it means without papers. We got papers."

~ ~ ~

Lillian had learned the meaning of the word at age fourteen. Outside her Uncle Pip's luncheonette in Flushing, New York, a man had yelled the slur from a passing car. She confided in her uncle, a striking figure who, at five-foot-ten, wore a thick mustache the same dark shade as his greased-back hair. "Kids call me that awl the time," she said.

Pip's face had grown crimson, "We ain't wops." He stared at the dusty exhaust of the unknown enemy before handing over the folded, brown paper bag. "Now, get." Pip patted Lillian's behind as she turned to deliver neighborhood bets to the address scratched on the back of a torn lunch ticket. The package contained numbers for the community lottery, a mob-backed gambling racket where area players paid a couple of bucks to guess three digits, hoping to match the winning numbers. Payouts were small, and profits were large for the men who ran the neighborhood draw.

Holding her tongue and the precious bets close to her chest, she scooted off in her saddle shoes, skipping from the luncheonette, and ignoring catcalls of the men on the bench out front. Silence was not Lillian's forte, but fear sealed her lips whenever she passed numbers for her uncle. Fear of her father's belt and ten dollars for delivery was worth her quiet.

~ ~ ~

Joe straightened his buckle, "What about lunch Wednesday? I'm off."

"Sure. Where?" Lillian wrung her hands. If Joe chose a place far from the neighborhood, she'd have to say no. Without bus fare, walking and hitchhiking defined the boundaries of her world.

"Lum's is good if you like Chinese. I could pick you up." Joe checked his watch. Break time was over. "Where you live?"

Lillian opened the flower-covered purse she'd borrowed from her mother, pulled out her skate rental receipt, and wrote down the address. She offered Joe the paper, letting her hand linger on his. He flinched, then gave her hand a sharp squeeze. "Cool, see you then, curly."

Lillian touched her hair self-consciously. "See ya." She followed Joe back to the hum of the rink. He nodded at her, heading back to the rental counter.

Lillian found her friend at the rail, leaning on Juan, a thick-muscled Puerto Rican whom Bella had crushed on for months. Juan wore a tired look of indifference.

"Come on, Bella, let's get outta here. Gotta tell you something."

"Sure." Bella looked back to say goodbye to Juan. He was gone.

"I got a date," Lillian proclaimed, bending to help Bella undo her skates.

"With coppo, doppo? You sure? He gave me the heebie-jeebies." Bella pulled a compact from her purse to touch up her Persian Melon lipstick. She pursed her lips with an audible smack.

"He's nice."

"Come on, I seen kinder eyes than that cop's on dem rotten fish floating under the bridge. Sometin's off."

"You're just jealous," Lillian offered, grabbing the skates for return. While she waited in the skate return line behind a well-dressed negro boy, Bella waited on the bench closest to the exit, picking the last bit of tangerine polish from her chewed nails.

Joe looked up when Lillian reached the counter, his nostrils flaring and teeth bared. His wrathful expression morphed into something resembling a grin as soon as he realized it was her. Blinking, she offered the skates, "Here you go." Joe's large hands unfolded in a welcoming gesture.

He took her skates, tucking in the leather tongues and laces to get them ready for the next renter. "Sorry about that. Some kid just threw me a bunch of skates at once. Nigger didn't even thank me."

"Oh. Um. Okay," she blinked rapidly.

"Nah, don't get me wrong. They're alright, so long as they don't get uppity. He had a problem. You all set?"

8

"Yes. Thank you," Lillian smiled. "See ya Wednesday."

Bella waited at the front door. "What's up, buttercup?"

"He seemed upset. A negro returned a bunch of skates or something."

"Huh? What did he say?"

"Nothing. Never mind." Lillian changed the subject. "Your parents gonna give us a ride?"

"Think so. Babo read me the riot act, but he'll be here. We better go. He hates waiting."

"Yeah, hot in here anyway." Lillian looked back at the skate rental station where Joe filed skates into cubicles by size. Turning to wait on another customer, he caught her watching him. Slowly, he lifted a hand to wave. Lillian waved back.

"Let's go." Bella shoved Lillian towards the exit, watching Joe, who, leering, raised a hand to his lips to blow Lillian a kiss.

2 Settlers

One thousand one hundred seventy-two miles separated my adoptive ancestors before they emigrated through the hopeful yearning of Ellis Island to New York City in the early 1900s. As the Barbiera and Selbach families first stepped onto American soil, an overabundance of everything defined the place where Times Square billiard halls rumbled with broken English, and the Statue of Liberty wore a dull brown copper color that would take another twenty years to turn green.

My adoptive grandfather, Josef Selbach Senior, emigrated from Friedberg, Bavaria, Germany, in 1929, while on my adoptive mother's side, great-grandfather Francesco Barbiera made his way from Palermo, Sicily, around 1900. Each traveled in the feces stench of steerage where a cross-Atlantic ticket cost thirty bucks, and dreaming was free. They arrived with hopeful hearts, little money, and a dream that they would thrive in the immigrant-rich city.

Hope for better circumstances defined their journeys and, ultimately, mine.

~ ~ ~

On the night Joe met Lillian's Sicilian family for the first time, she watched for Joe's arrival from the living room window of her parent's house. Hiding behind the thick drapery so her father would not discover that she was going on her sixth date with Joe, she fidgeted, anxious about what Rosario Barbiera might say to her police officer boyfriend. Lillian's father was soft-spoken but hot-tempered. When his only son Jim snuck out at night, departing from the metal fire escape where his children often slept in summer, Rosario ignored it. When his daughter did the same, the punishment was swift and painful.

Rosario, the third of six brothers raised at East 136th Street, did not venture far from the South Bronx after marriage, living in the borough until a flood of violent crime and racial tension turned the neighborhood dangerous. In search of safety and opportunity, Rosario moved his wife, son, and daughters to Bayside, Queens, in 1953.

It was there, in the four-story building where her father worked as a superintendent, in addition to his jobs at Krug's Bakery and as a mail sorter for the post office, that Lillian hid. Watching Joe's green car pull up to the curb, her stomach tingled with excitement. Hoping to avoid a parental inquisition, she raced down the stairs before Joe's foot could touch the sidewalk. Carefully opening the door, she tried to sneak out unnoticed.

Joe had other ideas. He pushed his way into the small entry hall, trapping her between the men who would come to define her life. Rosario loomed at the top of the stairs, hands tucked into the pockets of charcoal dress pants, jingling the loose change he always carried.

Lillian yelled up to him, "Daddy, this is Joe. We won't be late."

"How ya doin?" Joe nodded.

"I'd be better if dem poliziotto friends a yours stopped haulin' my family to the can. Ain't a crime ya know, being Italian."

Joe shrugged his shoulders. "Bums a bum, as far as I see it."

Rosario's face reddened. "Be careful, Lillian." He squinted, sizing up Joe's intentions, and the men shared a gape-mouthed moment of appraisal.

"We're okay. See ya later, Daddy," she yelled up the mahogany staircase, slamming the door before her father could answer.

A single black cloud does not signal a hurricane. But, even from as far away as the in-between, I knew Lillian would need an umbrella. Full of infractions and a million ways they might avoid them, each romantic interlude pointed to the inevitability of the thunder to come.

Lillian stared out Joe's car window as they pulled into the parking lot across from the restaurant. Neighborhood twenty-somethings spiffed up in their Sunday best packed the Bell Boulevard eatery. Thin waiters in bowties circled the joint with large trays and helpful expressions. A ten-deep line of eager customers snaked from the door of the popular date place out onto the sidewalk. "Reservations," Joe repeated twice as they squeezed past the line.

Joe held her shoulder, escorting her past the crowd. He pulled out her chair once they reached the table. Lillian's eyes widened when she saw the "reserved" sign next to a vase of long-stemmed red roses. None of the surrounding diners had flowers. Lillian, whose typical dates consisted of malt shop feel-ups and park bench make-outs, beamed.

"Bring us a bottle of bubbly," Joe demanded in the sarcastic tone reserved for anyone who served him. "And two of dem veal specials. You like veal, right?" Unsure, Lillian nodded.

The waiter returned quickly to deliver two champagne flutes and pour. Joe lifted his glass, toasting awkwardly, "To, uh, the way it's gonna be."

Lillian thought she might cry, feeling the same dread and freedom as when her father found out she had been cutting high school for months.

"You like being a cop?" she sipped her drink, wiping the tickle of the bubbles from her nose.

"Yeah, I like locking up assholes who laugh too loud," Joe announced, his attention fixed on the table next to them, where two soldiers snickered and snorted alongside their comely dates. The laughter stopped when they heard Joe's comment. One of the men started to stand, and his girlfriend, a wavy redhead, touched his hand, shaking her head. Satisfied that he had muzzled their annoying racket, Joe turned back to Lillian.

"Evva been here?" Joe asked, leaning back, clasping his hands behind his neck. She shook her head.

Lowering his hands, he smirked, "Couple of my buddies told me 'bout it. Classy joint. Too bad they let dat trash in." Joe raised his shoulder, indicating the soldiers.

Lillian glanced sideways at the attractive women and their uniformed dates, who glowered at Joe as he kept talking, oblivious to the heat rising in the soldier's faces. "Heard it was some kinda palace, but you gotta wonder wid that element."

The waiter arrived, standing between the parties to block Joe's view, and delivered the soldiers their receipt. He gestured towards the door. "No trouble," he cajoled, smiling ingratiatingly. "Thanka you so much. Thanka you. Good night, okay?"

Due to the romantic coaxing of their dates, who pecked cheeks and whispered inspirations to hasten their departure, the soldiers agreed it was time to go. The waiter followed the foursome to the door, holding it open for them to exit.

Joe wore a triumphant look, despite the server's low-browed head shake as he passed. Lillian wondered what Joe had against the group until her porcelain-plated dinner arrived. She bowed her head, giving thanks for the meal.

Joe ignored the prayer, slicing the thin meat like a surgeon retrieving a kidney. He placed the first slice between his teeth before seeming to inhale it with an audible slurp. They ate in silence. Except for the din of other diner's conversations and the clinking of ice against metal jugs as waiters filled glasses, all they heard was chewing.

After dinner, Joe held Lillian's hand as he drove her to Crocheron Park, a popular make-out spot between 214th Street and 35th Avenue. A fog of lusty body heat obscured the windows of the cars to the right and left of the car.

Joe yawned; reaching across the back of the seat, he snaked his arm around her soft shoulder. With the other hand, he produced a small diamond ring. She covered her mouth in surprise.

"So, you wanna get hitched?" Joe asked, sliding the ring onto Lillian's already extended ring finger.

"Oh, my Gawd, yes." She watched Joe's eyes to see if her short finger would garner a look of disgust. She was born without a knuckle on her left ring finger, and the doctors informed her parents that surgically attempting to repair the deformity would have rendered the finger useless. Joe smirked as he slipped the ring on her hand, kissing her hard to seal the deal. He did not mention her deformed digit.

Lillian admired the ring, holding it up to the rear-view mirror to admire its glistening reflection. "Oh, Joe. I can't believe this. Me, getting married. I'll be Mrs. Joe Brooks. Lillian Brooks, the wife of a state trooper."

"About that," Joe pulled her closer, moving his face within inches of hers. "Now, don't get dramatic. I'm gonna tell you some-din that don't mean anything, okay? Promise not to blow a gasket?"

The park light flickered behind them, revealing Joe's worried expression. His face appeared sinewy, ominous. Lillian backed up, dreading whatever was about to ruin her marriage proposal.

"What?" she asked, holding her breath, expecting the worst.

"I told you my name was Joe Brooks at the rink 'cause that's the name I use at da job." His tone sounded rehearsed, like he'd practiced the statement for hours.

14

Confused, she asked, "What? That's not your name?" Her hand reached for the door handle as she considered dodging Joe and his made-up name. But she sat still, cemented by a more considerable peril than Joe's lie, that this would be her lone chance at marriage.

Headlights entered the park, and Joe paused to watch a bright red Cadillac pull onto the dirt before continuing the awkward introduction. A section of his gelled hair fell forward, and Joe slicked it back before announcing, "Name's Selbach. Joe Selbach." He looked at her as if she should applaud. Lillian stared back, still silent. "I use da name, Brooks. Lots of guys change their names, in case the whole dating thing don't work out. Dames ain't right in the head sometimes."

Lillian's heart stopped. Dumbstruck, she processed the lie. She wondered if this was the marriage she deserved—whether it might be divine punishment for running numbers for her uncle and dropping out of school.

She considered jogging to the Thirty-One bus stop near the White Castle. She had two choices, catch a bus back to the room she shared with her sister or give Joe Brooks a little leeway.

Joe continued the bombardment of truths. "I'm not a state trooper either. I'm an ironworker. I didn't tell the rink boss 'cause of all the union crap. I needed cash during the layoff. So, when we met, I just told ya the same ding. I didn't know you yet. Had to make sure you wouldn't yap to the boss."

"Joe, I... prove it," she shrilled, reeling around to face him full on. "Prove that's your real name. It's been two months. I can't believe... how come you didn't tell me?" Her head ached. She grew tongue-tied from the enormity of the lie.

Aggravated by her uneasiness, Joe retrieved his wallet from his back pocket. He removed his license and union card from the brown leather fold, handing them to Lillian to prove his identity. As he did, a photo of a young boy fell on the seat between them. Joe scooped it up quickly, "Dat's nothin. Just my Godkid." He tucked the photo back into his wallet. "But looky here, see, I'm telling ya the truth," he reassured, puffing out his lips and tilting his head. "I swear. It don't matter. Look, I got a good-paying job, just not the one I said."

Lillian understood the need for lies. A truth-bender herself, she fibbed copiously to save herself from her father's belt. When she looked at the man who would become her fiancé that night, she did not judge him or run, deciding instead to overlook his dishonesty.

She handed Joe's crinkled license back. Trying to appear strong but desperate to keep Joe hooked, she asked, "Anything else you want to tell me?"

"No, Lillian. I swe-ah," he explained in a phony-sounding plea. "It was just a work thing. Now, get over here, Mrs. Selbach. Give your fiancé a smooch."

Joe put his hands on her arms, pulling her close, and her hand slipped from the sweat-coated door handle. Joe kissed her, and she responded. Judgments of his deceit evaporated along with the lies that forged them. The car's windows clouded, obscuring the view and hiding the half-truths that would define their engagement, marriage, and life. Neither Lillian nor Joe attempted to remove the fog.

3 Matrimony

What is the worldly opposite of murder? Some would answer birth. But for me, it is the budding romance of mutual love. Weddings represent a hopeful bloom as delicate and intricate as fine Italian lace. Every flower, frill, and nuance associated with exchanging vows fans my heart's happiness. Weddings are the only occasion when souls alight in delicate beauty and tears of happiness drip on aged and fresh cheeks alike. I adore wedding stories except for this one.

My adoptive mother told me the story of her wedding day with a joyful glint in her eye. We were alone in her Savannah, Georgia, apartment. A yapping Yorkie across the hall barked as visitors passed through the hotel-like corridor of the senior apartment building. Her apartment's combined living room, dining room, and tiny kitchen seemed too small for all the memories I pulled from her with my pointed questions. The apartment walls were lined with photos of survivors, mostly children...hers, mine, and my brother's.

My adoptive parents' wedding story is a tragedy to me, so I could not help but be fascinated by my mother's ability to look back at the day she married Joe with a measure of amusement. Whether her smile as she retold the story was a sign of strength or the softened edges of memory loss, it made me understand the resiliency of aging. She finds the good in what would be defined by most as awful—an essential survival skill.

~ ~ ~

It was November 28, 1961, three months after she met Joe at the roller rink. Lillian, Joe, and her father, Rosario, had been waiting twenty minutes for the officiant to return from a coffee break. She closed her eyes against the harsh fluorescent light of the county clerk's office.

When she opened them, the room seemed softer. Drinking in the faint luminescence, she looked around, hoping the court secretary had lit a candle. She inhaled, searching for a whiff of the beeswax she associated with a Catholic mass. Her father gave her a calm wink from the leather chair reserved for family and witnesses, and Lillian searched for the non-existent candle. The light in the room was the same, as was Joe's bored expression.

Rosario stood. Straightening his thin black tie, he moved closer to whisper, "Your mudder will be awlright wid dis as soon as we get home. Don't you worry, Lilly."

On the day after Lillian announced her engagement, Helene Barbiera had informed the family that she would never attend her daughter's wedding to "that man." She disliked Joe from the moment they met.

The court clerk, a giant of a man, returned to the room. Smiling at Lillian, he placed his glasses atop his nose to inspect the pile of marriage paperwork on the counter that separated him from betrothed couples. Moving to a podium set in the corner of the room for such occasions, he waved at Joe, indicating that it was time to start.

Over Joe's shoulder, Lillian glimpsed the glisten of a spider's web growing long and wide in the court window. Locating the eight-legged creator undulating from a silken thread, she winced at its quarter-sized body and menacing pincers. Horrified, she pulled Joe closer, choosing the venom she knew.

The clerk, misinterpreting Lillian's clingy posture as desire, assured her. "Just a minute more, and you'll have him all to yourself." The stooped giant smiled as his secretary returned to the chamber.

"Looks like we're ready. Thank you for being patient. I see we have the license. Is this your witness?"

Rosario nodded.

"Good. Then if you'll step over here."

Lillian took Joe's hand which felt clammy. She wondered if her fiancé was nervous.

"Lillian Barbiera, do you take Joseph Selbach as your lawfully wedded husband?"

She looked at Joe, who stared straight ahead, and then at her father, who grinned the same slanted grin he always wore during a belt whipping. "I got to teach you kids right from wrong. But I love you, Lillian," he would say.

Lillian wondered if this was a lesson she needed to learn and whether Joe's painful dishonesty at the start of the relationship was a similar kind of love. "I do," she told the clerk. Joe looked at his watch before repeating his vows.

It was over as fast as the clerk predicted. Lillian became Mrs. Joe Selbach without the blessings or pomp of her religion. She smiled, despite the brevity of the civil procedure, but secretly mourned the lack of well-wishers to send them off in a shower of rice.

At the podium, under the watchful eye of her father, she looked back on the web. A cloud passed over the sun, rendering the silky snare invisible without its glistening backlight. She exhaled, relieved by its temporary invisibility.

Joe paid the clerk, peeling four crisp bills from his wallet.

"Congratulations!" the secretary exclaimed, offering a thick sheet of paper.

"Yeah." Joe grabbed the marriage certificate with its embossed seal in one hand and Lillian's elbow in the other. As Joe rushed her from the small room, another couple entered the chamber, hanging onto each other like fruit on a tree. He wanted to avoid a ticket on the car, which he'd parked on a flat patch of grass, saying, "Not legal, but good enough."

Lillian wore a tight smile as they entered the great hall outside the chamber. Slowing her pace to let Rosario catch up, she hoped Joe would show her some affection in front of the couples waiting for their turn at nuptial bliss.

"Congratulations!" a young woman with black hair and a veiled pillbox hat exclaimed as Joe towed Lillian past the line. "We're next," the willowy woman bubbled, caressing her fiancé, who embraced her with smug certainty.

Lillian frowned at the plainness of her wedding, wondering if it was her penance for Joe's previous marriage to the woman he called "Penny the Nag." For Joe, where they got married seemed inconsequential, and he did not seem interested in church donations or other frivolous fees related to getting hitched. When the priest informed them that his divorced status forbade him from getting married at Saint Dominic, he'd chuckled, "Well, ain't that grand, Padre. If I ain't good enough for this dump, screw it."

"We have to stop at my house to drop Daddy off," Lillian said once they reached the car. "I'll get my pillow and toothbrush too. Don't have anything at your apartment."

"All right. But make it quick." Joe turned the key in the ignition, looking over his shoulder to back up. Rosario shook his head at Joe's half-hearted attitude. Lillian laid her hand on Joe's. He recoiled. "Driving here," he snapped, squashing her excitement.

Lillian bounded up the stairs of her parents' home, taking two steps at a time. She found her sister Helen in the front room listening to Dion croon "Runaround Sue" on the console radio. "Hey," she said, but her sister barely looked up from the *Dig Magazine* she was reading.

Trying to catch her breath, Lillian screeched, "I got news. Where's Mom?"

"She's cooking. Where's the fire, spaz?"

"Mind your beeswax. Where'd you get a quarter for a *Dig* flake?"

"Roberta gave it to me. She's gonna give me the Elvis Army issue next. Might let you read it." Helen peered over the cover with its artist rendering of Annette Funicello, her raven locks secured by a red hairband. "What gives?"

"Never mind. I gotta get with it. Joe wants to push off."

"Good. Weddings make me hungry," Rosario arrived, his hand rubbing his rumbling stomach. Joe stepped into the parlor next.

"I'll get her, Daddy." Lillian bounced to the bedroom she shared with her sisters, grabbing her toothbrush and a handful of underwear from the dresser's top drawer. She threw the items into a pillowcase and laid it at the head of the stairs before going to the kitchen.

While Lillian packed her things, her mother had joined Rosario in the parlor, where she wore a studied look of inconvenience. Rosario poured whiskey into two tumblers and started to grab a third. Helene shook her head. "I can't drink when I cook. You want it burnt? So, what's so toast-worthy."

Joe accepted the glass, wearing the satiated look of a cat digesting a juicy mouse. It was the same look he had worn throughout the ceremony.

"It is, Mom," Lillian exclaimed. "We're married."

"What? Today?" Helene gaped at her husband, "How could you do this behind my back?"

Rosario answered in the calm tone reserved for his headstrong wife, "You never liked the man, Helene. Said you didn't want any part of it."

"Why wasn't I at your wedding? I'm your mother," she asked Lillian.

Lillian answered quietly, "Because you said you didn't want to go, Mom. You would have ruined the whole thing."

Helene turned to Joe, "You're right; I don't like him. He's not right for you."

Joe met her glance, unaffected. "Too late for dat, ain't it, Mrs. Barbiera?"

Rosario sprayed the golden liquor from his lips at the boldness of Joe's reply. Wiping the stickiness from his mouth, he stifled a laugh at his wife's reddening complexion.

"I should have bought plastic slipcovers," Helene scolded. "You men can't take a drink without dribbling all over my furniture."

"*Buona fortuna, mia figlia.* I hope you're happy." Rosario kissed Lillian's cheek, and she lifted the white gold and pearl wedding ring for his approval. Rosario clucked his tongue, studying it.

Helene embraced her daughter stiffly before heading back to the kitchen. "Be well; I hope it works out. I gotta stir the Fagioli. Stay for dinner if you want."

Joe pointed at his watch as the thin veil of sentimentality in the room evaporated. Lillian gathered her items, hugging her father before descending the long staircase. She looked back once. Rosario wore a contemplative mask. Lillian hesitated, turned around, and ran up the stairs to kiss his cheek.

Rosario grinned. "Get now, married lady."

The drive to Joe's apartment was knotted with silence. Lillian had been to Joe's one-bedroom apartment before. But arriving as man and wife tightened her chest and sealed her lips.

Joe opened the door. Smiling, she waited for him to lift her over the threshold. Joe picked up her pillowcase, shaking his head. "You waiting for Christmas? Get in here."

"I just thought you might, well..." She lingered a few more hopeful seconds.

"With this knee? Ain't hapnin," Joe said, amused. "Sooner you get in here, the sooner I get dinner."

Inside, Lillian laid the pillowcase on the counter. The three-room flat was neat, charmless, and about the same size as her parents' living room.

"It'll have to do until we find a bigger place." He picked up her case, and she nervously followed him to the tiny bedroom. The graying walls did not have a single decoration hung on them. Joe placed her case on the bed and pointed at the dresser. She opened each of Joe's drawers as he watched. Into the half drawer of space he'd cleared for her, Lillian emptied the case contents, folding each item neatly to match the pristine creases of Joe's things.

"It's fine. Shared a room with my sisters," Lillian reassured him. The lie added another stone to the mountain of squashed expectations that would come to define her memory of the day. "I wish someone from your family could have been at our wedding. I would have liked to have met your parents." Her glacial blue eyes stared into the bathroom mirror Joe used for shaving, but he did not answer. Sliding her toothbrush into the hole next to his, she looked from the tiny washroom to see if he was listening.

When Joe finally spoke, he used a placating tone that made her feel silly. "I told you, no family to speak of and no need to get everyone all worked up. Now, how about dinner, wife?"

23

4 Invasion

Two years before my birth, my soon-to-be adoptive mother's biggest worry was filling the free time that came with being a wife. Like all the beautiful *befores* that life delivers, they are miraculous for their obliviousness. Just two months into the marriage, my mother was finding her way despite the questions that swirled in her head. Why would Joe's family get "worked up" about their marriage? Was it that she was Italian? Catholic? Not good enough?

Decades later, when I asked Mom about the early days of the marriage, she shifted in the baby blue recliner that matched her eyes and eased the fibromyalgia that caused her near-constant pain. The wrinkles of Mom's forehead deepened under the baseball cap she wore to hide how her once thick curls had straightened from her battle with breast cancer. The answers Mom sought as a young bride had arrived like a meteor.

~ ~ ~

Joe was at work, pounding iron atop the Verrazano Narrows double-decked suspension bridge that would soon connect the Brooklyn and Staten Island boroughs. Lillian had sent him off before dawn and, after a half-hour cat nap, got busy rearranging the linen closet that Joe had complained was "a damned tragedy" the night before. On her knees, she had just emptied the contents of the bottom shelf when the doorbell rang. She rose, stretching her back and kicking aside the mound of hand towels to answer the bell.

Lillian peered through the eyehole and, unable to make out the face of the visitor, opened the door. Standing there was a short, ashen lady so immense that her sides disappeared outside the door frame. Lillian gasped at the woman's size, covering her mouth at the rudeness of her reaction. The visitor did not notice, staring grim-faced into the apartment.

The woman had the unabashed presence of a steamroller. A large kidney-shaped stain adorned her plaid dress, and bunched-up stockings engulfed her ankles. Behind her, mostly obscured, appeared her physical opposite, a skeletal kid with a golden waterfall of hair. The boy wore thick eyeglasses and looked bored. Under Lillian's scrutiny, he tucked a few locks of hair behind his ear.

"Where's Joe?" The stranger asked as she pushed Lillian aside, squeezing into the apartment. "I got to sit down." Her accent was a dialect that sounded to Lillian's untraveled ear like a German beer commercial imitating a New Yorker. "And who the fuck are you?"

Flustered, Lillian answered, "I'm Joe's wife."

The young man hung back in the hall as the woman blocked the doorway. "Joe's wife is Penny, and his son's Tommy," she screeched, crooking her neck and narrowing her eyes at the slipcovers Lillian bought to spruce up Joe's hand-me-down furniture. "They're separated. That's why he moved to dis dump."

Lillian caught her breath. "Joe has a son?" she mumbled, the face of the little boy in the photograph Joe had dropped the night of their engagement coming into focus. Was that him? By then, the sneering intruder had shuffled across the carpet. "I… who are you?" was all Lillian managed before the woman's gag-inducing aroma of sweat and Crisco made her choke.

25

"Well, ain't dis sometin, Karl?" She lowered herself on the dining chair, which creaked at the load. "I'm Millie Selbach. Joe's mudder," she said, scowling at the yellow frills of the curtains.

Lillian grabbed the chair nearest Millie for support, "His mother? I thought you were dea…" She did not finish the sentence as the reality of the lies settled in, choking her voice and heart.

The skinny boy pulled a chair from the table, nodding for permission before sitting across from his mother. "I'm Karl," he said quietly.

Lillian's mouth went dry with the shock. Mortified by the pile of towels she'd left on the floor, she blurted apologetically, "I was cleaning…. I never, and it doesn't usually look like this." Millie shrugged, studying Lillian, who paled at the intense dislike in her gaze.

"Would you like tea?" Lillian asked, eager to leave the room. She reached for the tap before Millie could react.

"No. Ve're not staying. Just no vord from Joe since Penny took off. Vas time to check on 'im. Guess you been keeping my boy from me." Millie looked past Lillian with disapproval at the flowered dishes that lined the open shelves. "Prettying da place up, yeah?"

"Yes, well. I, um…" Tongue-tied, Lillian turned off the water, licking at the gush of sweat on her upper lip.

Karl tapped his fingers, humming under his breath, seemingly immune to his mother's hostile tone. Millie stood, narrowed her eyes at Lillian, and snapped her fingers at Karl, who hurried to help her up. Without another word, she shuffled out the door sideways. Karl looked up, smiling a shy grin before following his mother into the hallway.

Lillian closed the door, breathless from the visit and the revelation of Joe's child. In a fog for the rest of the day, she folded every towel in the trifold method Joe had taught her. When every shelf was perfect, she stepped back to admire the systematic neatness of the results, a sharp contrast to the state of her mind.

When Joe returned from work that night, Lillian's interrogation ignited before he was in the front door, "Your mother was here, your brother too. You said your parents were dead. They didn't even know about me. You have a son? Where is he? My God, Joe, you shoulda told me. First, your name, now this. What else have you lied about?"

"You tell her we're married?" Joe probed; his foul mood heightened by the news of his mother's visit.

"Yeah, I had to. What was I supposed to do? That's what you're worried about? What about your son? Don't you want to tell me more about him?"

"Shit." Joe slammed his lunchbox on the nearest surface, stopping her mid-question. "Now we gotta go there." Joe kicked the chrome leg of the table, sending his lunch box clamoring to the floor. The sandwich remains scattered. His thermos bounced towards the sink, the glass inside shattering. A half-eaten apple rolled toward the icebox.

"Go where? What's going on?" Lillian leaned her head on her hand, waiting for his answer.

"None of your fucking business. Neider is my son. The bitch left. Took my kid. That's all you need ta know." Joe's eruption stopped Lillian from asking the questions that sounded in her head like a fire alarm.

"You didn't tell them we got married," she said, stooping to retrieve the remains of her lying husband's lunch. Brushing shards of lettuce and ham into her hand, she looked up.

Joe's cheeks puckered as he drew back his foot. She clenched her teeth, her eyes filling at the site of his strike-ready boot. The room grew hot with anticipation. "Please, Joe, don't," she whispered, tensing her stomach muscles for the attack.

He had threatened her once before. They were painting the bathroom she had insisted they update to a cheerful blue when she mentioned he'd missed a small section near the mirror. He threw the paintbrush hard at her head, missing and hitting a section of wall they had already painted. She had laughed it off, despite his angry expression.

"Hmmm. Maybe I will. Maybe I won't." Joe speculated, standing over her now; his foot raised a few inches above the floor.

Stomping his foot near her stomach, he kicked the rotten apple core at her mouth before stepping over her to get to the fridge.

"Thirst wins," he said, laughing and grabbing a Schlitz from the shelf. "Gonna watch the news. Clean this shit up, will ya?"

Lillian lay there for a minute, squeezing the brown flesh of the apple core until the last bit of juice ran through her fingers, puddling on the cracked linoleum. She watched as his flannel-clad shoulders disappeared into the living room. "He has a son," she whispered, rolling onto her back and finally allowing the tears to come.

5 Garbage Point

A few weeks after Millie and Karl Selbach invaded, my soon-to-be mother and father drove past the old movie theater turned bingo hall and the colorful awning of the Butcher Shop to Joe's childhood home at 124-11 20th Avenue in College Point.

A predominately German town in Northeastern Queens, College Point is named for the long-defunct St Joe's College. Built along the East River in 1850 on land chosen for its spectacular views of Manhattan, the college closed after fifteen years.

College Point had a reputation for its odorous refuse. The primarily residential area's remote location and a large trash incinerator engorged at its center earned the name "Garbage Point." It was a dumping ground for the city's unwanted things. One of a dozen tightly spaced houses, the Selbach abode was a singular structure, its drab existence defined by drawn shades and dangling rain gutters.

~ ~ ~

Swatting at a buzz of black flies, Lillian side-stepped the mashed remains of an oozy cantaloupe while holding a Jell-O concoction close. Layered orange slices and mini marshmallows topped the mountain-shaped mold, and the dessert jiggled as she walked.

As she moved past the smashed remains of a child-size guitar, an emaciated kitten darted from a nearby trash pile, unsettling a clatter of aluminum cans. Stumbling on a rise in the uneven cement, she nearly dumped the Jell-O.

Joe did not knock, entering through two closed doors and up the narrow stairwell. At the top, Joe reached over his wife to turn the black doorknob.

It was clear to Lillian that Millie Selbach took no pride in her home as the door swung open. A pile of cardboard boxes blocked the entrance, forcing them to use giant arching steps to make their way into the living room. Yellowed newspapers, cups, and half-eaten meals covered every surface. Relief from the street odor was short-lived as the stench of unwashed occupants followed her into the room.

Lillian braced the Jell-O mold firmly against her waist before presenting it to Joe's mother, who sat at the center of the mess. Millie nodded towards the kitchen.

She carried the showpiece dessert through the small doorway. A slight man in his mid-forties worked at stirring what looked like a skinny rubber tire in the boil of a large pot. Joe's father, Josef Senior, looked up briefly, turning back to the pot in time to smack back the eel's slithering attempt at escape.

Placing the dessert on the counter, she slunk away from the death smacks of the spoon against metal. In the living room, Millie grimaced when Lillian moved aside a yellow shirt to make room for herself on the couch. Raising her wrist to her nose, Lillian sniffed the cologne she'd applied for the special occasion, but the foul aroma fought back, lifting its stink quotient as she sank into the thick sofa cushion.

Joe sat next to her, oblivious to the floral dress beneath him. "Well," he explained, diving into the topic he knew his mother was seething about, "Penny took Tommy. Whore got my car too."

Millie spit at the puke-colored carpet, "Dat's my grandson, ya know?"

"Yeah, Ma. He's my son," Joe countered in an equally biting tone.

"Where'd you find this one?" Millie asked in German.

Lillian grew confused as the conversation wavered between English and German. Shifting on the couch, she raised her eyebrows, hoping for some clarification from Joe, but he ignored her.

"Abendessen," the small, muscular man yelled. Two doors off the dining area opened in unison. Lillian stood, following Joe's lead. It was time for dinner.

Joe's brother, Karl, arrived wearing headphones; the long black stereo cord snaked under his bedroom door. Sisters Anna and Lena flanked him, smiling the first Selbach smiles Lillian had seen since her arrival.

"You the second wife?" Lena asked, twirling a sunshiny curl with her pinkie.

"Of course she is," Anna interrupted. "We're his sisters."

Lillian watched in horror as Joe's father yanked the finally dead eel from the pot. Slicing it down the middle, he served it alongside boiled red cabbage and dumplings. Joe's sisters filled their plates, withdrawing to the room they'd shared since birth. Karl remained, tapping his foot to the music and grinning as he helped himself to the last of the dumplings.

Joe's parents spoke German throughout the meal and pointed at Lillian amid full-bellied laughter. She kept her head down; her ears perked for the moment they'd switch back to English.

When the heavy meal and exclusive dialogue ended, Lillian stood to help with the dishes.

"Leave that crap to my sisters. I want you to meet my grandmother," Joe ordered.

Joe's grandmother, Klára, lived down a narrow flight of stairs in the same three-room apartment Joe had shared with Penny in the first months of marriage. Joe knocked lightly on the door, and his grandmother responded with a bold "Eintrag."

A bleachy aroma mingled with the smell of freshly baked apple pastry made the basement air lighter and fresher than upstairs. Klára's expression lit up like a Macy's holiday window when she saw her grandson.

Klara ignored Lillian, except to nod when Joe told her in German that he had remarried and that Lillian was his wife. Klara fawned over Joe, served him a warm beer, and made space for him to sit beside her. Joe looked happy.

"When I was a boy," Joe told Lillian, "I spent most of my time down here, and Großmutter liked to dress me up like a little girl. My best memories from dis dump."

Lillian looked confused. "You let her dress you up?"

"Yeah, we danced like idiots to old polka music." He repeated what he said in German to his grandmother. Despite arriving from Hungary via Poland forty years earlier, Klara understood little English. Her laugh filled the small space, a loud bark that was at once happy and disturbing. Waddling to the Victrola, she blew a cloud of dust from its cover. Then, lifting the heavy lid, she placed a record on the turntable. The considerable heft of her stomach lurched forward with each crank of the handle. A jaunty, upbeat tune filled the room, and Klara bowed to Joe.

The record, an Octoberfest Classic, was warped with age. Standing to take his grandmother's weathered hand in his, he spun her once around the room in as grand a gesture as Lillian had ever seen her husband make. The couple took a second twirl around the parlor as the album caught, skipping. Joe's grandmother fell into her chair, upsetting a neat pile of magazines on the settee.

"Ha. Good times. I was happy here," Joe announced in a manner that indicated that no other place would ever usurp these memories. An uncharacteristic joy turned his cheeks crimson.

"Fun." Lillian's eyes widened.

"You'll always be ma best girl." He delivered a long kiss on his grandmother's shining forehead. Klara swatted him away with the magazine she had picked up to fan herself.

The visit ended with tears and their German conversation making Lillian feel like a pigeon jostling for a tiny spot in the wake of vultures.

"I enjoyed your family," Lillian lied on the ride home.

"Yeah, they're alright," Joe said, honking the horn at a cab driver who sped past as they maneuvered from the curb.

"One thing. I wonder if your family would mind speaking more English when I'm around. Confused the heck out of me."

"Yeah, well, they speak German," he scoffed, shaking his head and looking for the quickest route home.

6 Deceitful Dodger

My mother recalls her first year of marriage as busy and mostly contented. They moved from Joe's tight bachelor apartment to a newer building in Douglaston. In the classier Queens neighborhood, Lillian enjoyed setting up their new apartment and, aside from an occasional twinge of boredom when Joe was at work, felt tranquility settle over the marriage. Lillian loved cooking for and being close to Joe and complimented him often. They rode a slow-moving current of calm until the first tsunami washed over their marital journey.

~ ~ ~

Lillian folded the last work shirt from Joe's wash pile. Being under strict orders to press every fold made her feel useful. She sniffed at the fresh scent of the fabric. A surprising number of rules accompanied her marriage vows, but Lillian found contentment in her daily duties.

The sound of the fan mingled with Sinatra's crooning from the red plastic radio on the windowsill. Lillian laid the shirt atop the neat pile of matching garments and yawned. She placed her right hand above her stomach, hoping her sudden fatigue was a sign of her womb's condition. She whispered a prayer, "Lord, let this mean I am pregnant."

She set the kettle on the stove and gathered the pile of clean shirts. Sliding them into the cedar-lined drawer, she gave them a final pat just as the doorbell rang. Before answering it, she closed the drawer and straightened her wavy hair.

Two men in slick, black suits stood outside the door, their faces solemn. Assuming they were fundraisers, she said, "Good morning, would you like a cup of coffee? Sorry, all I have is instant."

The men exchanged perplexed glances. The light-skinned man scratched his clean-shaven chin before replying, "No, thank you, Ma'am. We're here to see Joe Selbach. Is he home?"

"No, Joe's at work." It was Lillian's turn for confusion. "Is something wrong?"

"When do you expect him?" the taller man asked.

"In an hour."

The blond agent pulled a wallet from the chest pocket of his tailored suit coat. His companion did the same. They flashed shiny silver badges in a single synchronized movement. She wobbled a bit when they announced, "FBI," in Dolby-quality stereo.

Satisfied that she understood who they were, the men lowered their badges and closed their calfskin wallets. "We'd like to wait. Would that be okay with you?"

Her nerves ramped up, moistening her palms. "Well, I don't think. I mean, shouldn't... What do you want?"

"Army business," the blond answered, casually sliding his hand into his pants pocket.

Lillian watched the swift movement, hoping he was not reaching for a gun. "My husband's not in the Army."

"Yes, we know. Can we wait inside?"

Pressure built in her head, "Yes. Sure. I guess so." She went to the kitchen, indicating to the men that they should wait in the living room. "I'll make the coffee."

The men took their places on the long couch as Lillian set the steaming cups on her hand-me-down Formica coffee table.

"If you'll excuse me, I'd like to make a phone call." She rushed to the bedroom, not waiting for an answer.

She dialed her parent's number, hands shaking. Helene picked up. "Barbiera residence."

"Mom, I'm scared. There are two FBI guys in the living room, and they say it's army business. What if Joe has to join the army? What am I going to do?"

Helene Barbiera, who had long ago given up on the idea of romance in marriage, sighed, "What we all do, Lillian. Shush up and support your husband."

"What if they send us far away? I've never been out of New York, and I don't want to move."

"Look, you're married. You just do whatever Joe wants. He's in charge. You'll be okay. It won't be forever. Nothing is."

She hung up. Sitting on the edge of the green satin bedspread, she listened to the murmur of the men talking in the next room. Kicking her feet and biting on her thumbnail, she waited for the sound of Joe's homecoming.

Twenty minutes later, Joe opened the apartment door. He looked around, expecting his wife to greet him. "Hey, Lillian, I'm home. Hustle your ass in here and get me a beer." Joe slammed his black metal lunchbox on the counter, slapping the truck keys down on the gold-flecked Formica.

"I'm in here. Some men are here to see you," she yelled from the bedroom.

Joe shook his head, unable to make out what she said, and headed to the living room.

When Joe began his wide stride across the room, the men were already standing. Before he could say a word, they had cuffed his

36

hands. The three men remained motionless, observing each other in a moment of suspended disbelief.

"What the fuck? Who are you assholes, and what are you doin' in my home?" Joe shook his cuffed arms in their faces, pulling his wrists apart until the chain grew taut.

"FBI, sir. You're under arrest for failure to enlist, and we'll be making a soldier of you today."

"Ma'am," one of the men moved toward the bedroom while the other held Joe's arm. "Ma'am, we'd like you to come out now to hear this, please."

Lillian obeyed but stopped in the doorway, a decent distance from the melee. She waited there, trembling from head to toe at the prospect of Joe's anger.

Joe seethed, raising his shoulders to exaggerate the force of his six-foot stature. "Don't say a word. You don't have to tell dese schmucks a thing," he said. Lillian nodded.

"No problem, Ma'am. You don't have to say anything. We need to inform you that your husband is under arrest, and we'll be turning him over to the United States Army. Joe Selbach failed to register for the draft and is now under federal order to report for duty." Her eyes widened, and Joe gave her a look of admonishment. Next, he spat on the bare wood floor and, wearing the same sneer of contempt he reserved for anyone in authority, jeered, "It ain't shit. I'll be back for dinnah."

The men grinned, apparently used to resistance far more physical than Joe's dirty looks. The blond agent handed Lillian the papers he'd been holding since his arrival. "Thank you," she whispered, looking away from the mix of pity and disgust in the officer's eyes.

"Sir, you're under arrest. You are to be delivered for service immediately. Once the enlistment process is complete, you will get one telephone call. You will use that call to inform your wife of your location."

The agents exchanged a winning look. Each grabbed one of Joe's shoulders, spinning him towards the door. Joe looked over his shoulder past Lillian. "Can't I at least take a shower? Some of us do real work." Joe looked at the agent's spit-shined shoes to his dirty work boots, raising an eyebrow at the evidence of their comfortable white-collar work.

"No, sir. You had plenty of time to prepare for enlistment. We'll be going now." The men linked arms with Joe, escorting him to the front door. Lillian was surprised at how they moved her six-foot husband as smoothly as floating a feather.

"I'll call you as soon as this bullshit gets settled," Joe said over his shoulder, wearing the same tight mask that Lillian's father wore before he beat her.

She grimaced, recoiling from the anger in Joe's eyes. "I'll be waiting."

Joe shoved his foot between the door and jam, leaving a skid mark, as the men thrust him into the hall and then closed the door behind them. Lillian retrieved a bucket of warm soapy water and a sponge before kneeling at the entrance to erase the evidence of Joe's attempted interruption of the FBI's retrieval.

"Lord, what will I do now?" Lillian stayed on her knees, praying for what seemed like an hour. She scrubbed at the stain until the paint underneath faded away to reveal the metal.

7 Head over Heels

Mom and Dad returned from the Peach State one month before the first beating. With an honorable discharge in his pocket, Uncle Sam no longer governed Joe's fists or feet. But freedom from service had a cost, and it was a charge my mother would pay in blood.

~ ~ ~

Arriving home from work, Joe slammed the door and his lunchbox. Lillian sat on the green loveseat, waiting to gauge his mood. The room smelled of heat and resin from the radiators she'd painted pale blue the day before.

Joe entered the room, peeling away the layers of work clothes he wore against the February wind. "Here," he said, dropping the items next to her for laundering and putting away. Lillian flinched, and his expression grew dim. He looked like someone wearing shoes two sizes too small.

"Take off your boots. I'll get you a beer," Lillian chirped, trying to sound cheerful despite the disappointing call from the Manhattan adoption agency. The woman from the agency had spoken plainly, "Due to the short duration of your marriage, we cannot approve you and your husband for adoption at this time."

"You think I want a God-damned cold beer after working out in that crap." Joe sat to remove his boots and socks, which he added to the pile of shirts. Spreading his spindly toes, he leaned forward to glare at Lillian. His eyes narrowed to snake-like slits.

Lillian picked up the heavy work coat, standing to shake the puddling of a few tiny icicles from the sleeves. She watched her husband in her peripheral vision, wondering what he was thinking.

Joe scanned the room next. His head cocked like a wary food inspector stuck in a grease trap dive. His eyes stopped on a coffee cup Lillian left on the end table in her haste to answer the agency's call. Joe grinned, puffing his lips in victory.

Lillian rushed to retrieve the cup, leaving the coat and shirts on the couch. Joe followed, standing in the door frame to watch her quickly rinse the cup and lay it on a towel to dry. The calmness of his scrutiny hastened her excuse-making.

"I forgot to get milk this morning. I'll just run down to the corner." She reached for her coat and hat on the wooden peg near the door. He pounced as she tugged on the second sleeve and opened the front door.

Joe's bare foot landed at the center of her lower back, propelling her down the steep stairwell. She grabbed for the railing but missed. She covered her head with her arms and felt the hard wood gouge her hip and back. Landing at the third step, she looked up.

Joe loomed in the doorway, his face contorted and fists raised while glaring at Lillian's crumpled body. A look of disappointment crossed his face when he realized his opponent was down for the count. Deflated, Joe lowered his hands, slamming the door on her pathetic predicament.

Lillian rubbed the throbbing ache in her leg as a shroud of shock descended, a convenient cover for the truth. She adjusted her torso, finding she could move her leg from its awkward position. Sitting against the lobby wall, she faced the line of metallic mailboxes.

She stared at the pink heart sticker bearing her and Joe's names. Decorating and baby-making had been on her mind the day she stuck it on the metal door. The sticker had signified hope for a happy life but now seemed presumptuous.

Unthinking, she touched her stomach in a hopeful way that had become a habit. She was sure another pregnancy would result in miscarriage. Despite the humiliation of losing four babies, she wanted another. A child would plug Joe's anger. She lay on the floor, rubbing her empty womb and hoping for another chance.

The slam of the apartment door got the attention of their downstairs neighbor Mrs. Murray. The kindhearted eighty-year-old opened her apartment door slowly, looking around to see what had caused her mother's wedding dishes to vibrate in the china cabinet. Spotting her young neighbor on the lobby floor, she hurried in a sluggish old lady rush to help.

"Oh, my, Lillian. Are you all right?" she asked, tugging Lillian's elbow to help her stand. Mrs. Murray's petite frame was too weak for the task, but her determined effort compelled Lillian to try harder. Once up, Lillian noticed the pain in her elbow and chin.

"You're bleeding, dear." Mrs. Murray produced a tissue under her sweater sleeve to dab at the cut next to Lillian's eye.

"I'm… I'm okay, Mrs. Murray, she murmured, her tongue thick and jumbled. "I lost my footing on the stairs. I can't seem to do anything right these days. I'm so sorry to bother you."

"That must have been quite a landing, young lady. My mother's dishes rattled like a San Francisco earthquake." Mrs. Murray's face was a lace-like maze of lifelines, and her delicate features melted in dismay at the idea of a single crack in her mother's World War II China.

"Yes, yes, it was. I was trying to retrieve the mail and…ow." Lillian rubbed around a raw spot on her elbow where the skin had peeled back.

"Shall I get your husband?" the widowed neighbor asked, turning towards the upstairs apartment. Her movement unleashed a refreshing waft of Vicks Vapor and aged cotton.

"No," Lillian declared too loudly. Mrs. Murray stopped, her lips puckered and brows raised.

"Isn't he home? I saw his truck?" Mrs. Murray tucked the soiled tissue under her sleeve, unaffected by its stained state.

"Yes, um…, he's in the shower." Lillian lied, afraid of how Mrs. Murray might react to the truth. "He isn't feeling well. But I'll be okay. Thank you, and I should get dinner. Probably burned to a crisp." She embellished the lie to make it more believable.

"Okay, dear." Mrs. Murray watched her climb the stairs and returned to her apartment once satisfied that Lillian was safe.

As soon as she heard Mrs. Murray's door clasp, Lillian sat on a step to consider her options. She knew from experience that snakes rarely struck twice, and Lillian hoped that the venom of the attack had sent Joe slithering off into sad reflection. It had been the same with her father. Wallowing regret followed every belt whipping.

Her mind wandered back to her parents' home with its close quarters and volatile nature. Joe was terrible, but his habit of taking her on actual dates to a movie and dinner made her feel elegant.

Before their marriage, she'd dated half a dozen pompadour-coiffed delivery men from the transit authority garage. The garage was a hub of repair for the city's buses and trucks. In a crowded waiting room that smelled of burnt oil and sweat, drivers lost wages as they waited for vehicles. A few spilled to the sidewalk, happy for diversion, especially a female one.

Lillian started hanging out at the garage after dropping out of high school. Roaming the streets for seven hours a day to avoid her father Rosario's belt, the transit guys occupied her days until the truant officer phoned him.

That's when the whipping she had feared became a reality. Cornered behind the gold sofa, she tried to make her father see her side. "Dad, she insisted, "I'm just not smart enough for school."

To her great relief and confirmed dismay, her father had agreed. "You got that right. You're not too bright."

Now, staggering up the stairs, Lillian opened the apartment door, taking a deep breath before tiptoeing into the apartment. A dull snore emanated from the living room. After washing the blood from her face, she righted the vinyl kitchen chair that had toppled during the attack.

The bruises on her leg, arm, and shoulder swelling to purple and red, Lillian opened the fridge to retrieve ingredients. Holding onto the refrigerator door like a crutch and trying not to put much weight on her damaged leg, she envied the dead, sightless fish that would be their dinner.

8 Priest Toss

Joe arrived home tired and agitated by all the race talk on the radio. Ripe for an outburst, he entered through a wafting aroma of spaghetti sauce. "Better be meat in that," he barked at Lillian's turned back.

She faced him, beaming. Nine hours of cleaning and television had bored her. Yet, she brimmed with excitement at the idea of telling him about the phone call. After several miscarriages, she was sure she would not become a biological mother. Aching for the purpose and healing maternity would bring, she had decided on adoption. She applied to Catholic Aid, who said she and Joe wouldn't gain approval because they failed to marry in the church. Undaunted, Lillian had secured a meeting with the priest anyway.

"Hi, hon," she leaned into caress Joe. Appearing repulsed, he turned his cheek when she tried to kiss him.

"Yeah," he said, hugging her back half-heartedly.

"How was your day? Hang on. I'll get you a beer." Her husband was not much of a drinker. Unlike the uncles she'd served at dinners in her parents' home, Joe drank for refreshment rather than escape.

"Getting colder. Gonna need another insulated jacket from Sears. This job's a whore."

"Sure, I'll order it tomorrow. Sit down; I missed you today."

"Why? What makes today different than any other frigging day?" Joe rubbed his hands, which wore the tell-tale callouses of daily manual labor.

"I heard back from Catholic Aid," Lillian blurted the news, grinning ear-to-ear.

"We going to church now?" Joe took a long pull at the beer.

"Haha you know what I mean. The woman called today about our adoption application. They said no at first but agreed to have the priest stop in tonight."

Joe slammed the beer down hard, "Damn it, Lillian, I just got home. I need a shower. What time?"

"He'll be here at seven. Please..., you know how much I want this," Lillian frowned, afraid he'd make her cancel the meeting.

"Yeah, yeah. Hurry up with my dinner. I'll get in the shower." Agreeing to anything that was not his idea was problematic for Joe, so Lillian took her husband's reply as a holy sign that they would soon be parents.

The doorbell rang as Lillian put away the last clean dish. Inspecting her spotless surroundings, she placed a plate of oatmeal cookies on the table. The apartment smelled of smoke from a dollop of cookie batter spilled on the oven rack. Despite the low temperature outside, she opened the sliding glass door to air out the burnt odor.

Joe answered the door, neatly dressed and doused in Old Spice. The priest stood five feet three inches but peered at Joe with the attitude of a much larger man. "Hello, Mr. Selbach? I'm here about the adoption."

"Yeah. Come in." Joe scowled. Not a fan of the church or diminutive men who acted too self-assured, Joe's temper simmered.

The frocked priest sat across from Lillian, who wore a flowered apron and a goofy expression of admiration. Her respect for the collar and the church behind it made her nervous. The priest took a warm cookie from the plate, biting it as he opened the black leather folder. Lillian looked at Joe, who stood bent like a vulture, ready to tear apart his prey. She gestured at the padded chair for him to join them.

Joe sat rolling his eyes as the priest chewed. Lillian watched cookie crumbs tumble down the priest's black shirt, grimacing as he brushed them to the floor. Joe frowned at the defilement of his linoleum.

"It says here you married outside the church and that Mr. Selbach was married once before." The priest clucked his tongue, shaking his head at Joe.

"Yeah. That's right," Joe's cheeks went red.

"Would you like some tea or coffee, Father?" Lillian offered.

The priest waved her question away as he focused on the contents of the application on the table. "Says here you can't have children of your own due to medical issues and that you are looking to adopt an infant."

Before she could answer, the priest closed the folder, his expression solemn. "As my office informed you, we're not sure we can proceed with your case. You're not top candidates with the previous marriage and this one outside the church. Most of our couples are Catholic and don't…" he paused, "have any previous transgressions."

"Let me get this straight; I shaved for you to tell us we don't qualify?" Joe's face constricted, his thin lips tight as he spoke, "All right, den. Thanks a lot, Padre." He stood. "I'll see you out."

"Hold on, Mr. Selbach," the priest answered. "You seem like nice people, and your income and housing meet our criteria. So, we may be able to come to some agreement." The priest grabbed another cookie, chomping down and spreading crumbs as he spoke.

"What does dat mean?" Joe clenched and opened his hand several times.

"Wait, Joe. Please hear him out," Lillian begged, her dejected slump straightening.

"Well, Mr. and Mrs. Selbach, if you should decide to donate to the church, we might be able to move your application to the approval pile."

"What?" Joe got up, towering over the priest who remained seated.

Wanting to hear him out, Lillian scooted from her seat to the one closer to the priest. "How much?"

"How much is too much to pay for the privilege of motherhood? I believe five hundred dollars would go a long way to making this a beneficial meeting. Of course, the money would cover agency expenses, and there'd still be the normal processing costs on top of that."

"You want us to pay you $500. What are you, a fucking car salesman?" Joe inhaled, his frame inflating with thunderous fury. Lillian cringed, recognizing the anger that overtook him whenever he felt cheated.

Before the priest could answer, Joe lifted the surprised man from the chair by his white collar and belt. "Goddamned shyster," Joe roared, tossing the stunned man across the room towards the patio door.

The ripping screen frightened the neighbor's cat off the porch. The flash of black and white and the loud thump of the priest's landing startled a passing pedestrian. Joe tossed the adoption folder next. The Selbach's application forms fluttered to the ground, misplaced stepping stones on the grass beyond the cement patio.

Lillian started to rise, then sat back down, unnerved by Joe's slamming of the glass door. A glint of light from a passing car illuminated the priest's sprawled form. A tiny flash of movement gave her hope that he was unhurt.

47

Joe unbuttoned the top button of his shirt, retrieving another beer from the fridge. "That about solves that shit," he said, leaving Lillian to sit staring at the plate of cookies as he retreated to the living room.

The click of the television and the blare of the evening news startled her from the shock of the scene that had unfolded. Positive Joe would come after her if she did not tidy up; Lillian grabbed the dish rag to wipe away cookie crumbs. She wrapped the leftover cookies in foil, dabbing at the tears that rolled down her cheeks. Placing the cookies in the bread box, she decided never to speak of the priest again.

9 Parenthood by Proxy

Mrs. Green wore red. Like a Christmas in July sales rep, she sparkled at the door of the Selbach's apartment in late summer 1965. The Children's Relief Society was the third adoption agency to visit them. After interviewing them, the first two agencies had deemed the Selbachs unfit to adopt an infant.

Lillian did not understand why the other agencies turned them down but assumed it had to do with her housekeeping. Joe was always telling them what a lousy job she did. So, she'd spent the day tidying, dusting, and praying they would pass inspection. Motherhood was on her mind every minute of every day. It was the ship that would save her from drowning in a marriage ripe with rules and bullying.

The apartment was warm, despite fans oscillating in every window. Lillian hoped it would grow cooler once the sun lowered over Flushing. New York was under a heat advisory as the first heatwave of 1965 sizzled for the third day.

Lillian paced, her forehead beading with sweat as she waited for the family worker to arrive. Joe watched the television, glancing at Lillian and checking his watch in an obvious manner.

She opened the door before Mrs. Green lowered her finger from the bell. The social worker announced her intentions in the same formal tone as the other agencies. Placing infants was a serious transaction with little room for sentimentality. "I'm from Children's Relief. We have an appointment about your adoption application."

"Yes. Yes. Please come in." Lillian escorted the raven-haired woman to the table, where she offered a slice of lemon meringue. Retrieving the iced tea pitcher from the fridge, she filled three glasses.

Joe turned off the television to join them; Lillian whispered a quick prayer that his temper would keep. He strolled in, wearing a thin-lipped expression that meant he was in a good mood or pretending to be. "Joe Selbach, good to meet ya."

"Nice to meet you. You have an attractive home." Mrs. Green enjoyed a long sip of tea before getting right to the point. "I've reviewed your application. Once I complete the home study, which, from the look of things, will be all right, we'll discuss the child."

"The child?" Lillian dropped her pie-filled fork, and a splash of meringue landed on her blouse. "I'm so sorry. Joe says I'm the clumsiest woman he's ever met." She wiped at the sticky residue, over-apologizing as she patted the spot with a paper napkin.

Joe looked at his wife, shaking his head at the stain she now wore on her white blouse. A sideward glance at Joe's tense expression convinced Mrs. Green that the couple was a frantic mess. "Now, now. It's fine. You're nervous. It is an exciting time. Let's discuss the living arrangements and enjoy our pie."

Taking out her pad, Mrs. Green asked, "Do you have a lease here?"

"Yes, one year." Lillian was no longer hungry—her appetite usurped by anxiousness. The prospect of passing the home inspection and hearing more about the child turned her mouth to a kiln.

"Two or three bedrooms?" Mrs. Green asked.

"Two." Lillian noticed Joe scrutinizing her and sat up straighter, suddenly aware of her bent posture. She slouched a lot, and Joe did not like it one bit.

"Is the child's room ready? May I see it?"

"Of course," Lillian stood, but Joe held a hand up, indicating that he would lead the tour. She wanted to show off her handy work in the baby's room but zipped her lip for the sake of their prospective child. Joe led them to the room where hope lived in paint and preparation.

"Yeah, we painted it last week." He pointed towards the room. Mrs. Green took another cooling sip before rising to follow him. Lillian trailed behind, straightening pictures on the wall as they passed.

"We picked a neutral color, so it would be appropriate for a girl or boy," Joe explained. The eight-by-twelve room was a sunny yellow with glossy white trim. The window wore a sash of circus clowns in red, yellow, and black hues.

"We didn't have time to get any pictures for the walls yet," Lillian piped over Mrs. Green's shoulder from the hall.

"It's perfect. Cheery." The social worker said, making another note on her interview pad.

"May I see the rest?"

Joe opened the empty closet. "We'll fill this up once we know what we're getting. Do we get to pick? You know, girl or boy?" He lowered his clean-shaven chin, a severe expression entering his closed eyes.

Afraid the question might seem picky, Lillian looked at Joe pleadingly. "No, remember Joe? We told them we would take either, as long as it is an infant." She chewed at her inside cheek, hoping the comment would not rile him up.

"Yeah, but a girl would be easier. I hope it's a girl." He shut the door, nodding at Mrs. Green as he waited for her to answer.

"Well," Mrs. Green looked across the hall, noting the pristine state of the lavatory. "I'm ready to discuss that now. We have a baby girl. Let's chat in the living room if that is okay."

Lillian fidgeted on the couch, butterflies flapping in her stomach as Mrs. Green explained. "We have a baby in foster care. We've had her since birth. Her birth mother signed papers releasing her, so she is ready for permanent release. We want to place her as soon as possible. When do you think you'll be ready for a baby?"

Lillian could not believe she heard the question. She had been ready for months. She looked at Joe, trying to gauge how he was taking the information, "Now?"

"Yeah, why not?" He shrugged as if the woman had offered an extra slice of meatloaf. Joe was in no danger. For him, the parental role was utility rather than the necessity Lillian knew it to be.

Mrs. Green's expression softened at the couple's acceptance, and she appeared relieved, like she'd checked a giant mark off her to-do list.

"That is good news. The baby we are offering you has been in four foster homes since birth. We moved her often to be sure she would not bond with the non-custodial guardians. She is now eight months old, and we'd like to get her placed as soon as possible. You can meet her if you'd like to come to the agency tomorrow."

"Of course," Mrs. Green lowered her tone to indicate the solemnity of her following statement. "If you find her unacceptable for any reason, we'll find you another."

"Another? No, I mean, what time should we come?" Lillian beamed at the prospect of motherhood. She could not imagine the concept that any child might be unacceptable.

"How about 9 a.m.? We will have the baby brought to our Manhattan office on Third Avenue."

"We'll be there," Lillian blurted, covering her mouth when Joe looked her way.

"Yep. That works," he answered, standing up.

Gathering her things and thanking the Selbachs for their time, Mrs. Green left wearing a satisfied expression. As soon as the door closed behind her, Lillian pirouetted in celebration. A top released from a child's hand; she spun a colorful dance of delight.

"A girl, Joe. What should we call her? I like Helene for my mother, but then there's Rosie for Dad. I don't want her name to be ordinary. If it was a boy, I wanted to name him after Grandpa. Peter has always been my favorite. What do you think?"

"I think you should shut up and clean up," Joe barked jokingly. Lillian jumped when he swatted at her butt on his way to the fridge.

Taking a beer from the icebox, Joe left her to her daydreaming. "I'm gonna catch some news before bed. Don't be long. We gotta make a baby tonight."

Placing the iced tea back in the fridge, Lillian noticed the lid from the leftover sauce askew. Righting it, the childhood aroma of oregano made her think of her parents and how they would react to the baby.

Telling them about the adoption applications was clumsy. Their lack of experience with adoption made the conversation brief. With an exaggerated wink, her father Rosario asked only one question, "What if it's not Italian?"

Wiping sauce from the tablecloth, she imagined the eyes of her child. Joe seemed calm at the prospect of parenthood. A sure sign the baby would heal the marriage.

Eight hours of pretending to sleep later, Lillian went to her baby's room, where she stared at the circus clown curtains, wondering how much time they would have to get a crib. They had purchased a used mahogany crib at the onset of her first pregnancy. It was a beautiful piece of furniture that became a symbol of her failure to produce a viable life. She gave it to a neighbor the day after she suffered the agony of her first miscarriage. She wept with joy at the idea of purchasing a new crib for the child she felt she'd waited a lifetime to meet.

Lillian decided they would buy a white crib if granted permission to adopt the baby girl. A white crib would mean a fresh start for her marriage and their child. Joe entered the room, observing Lillian's teary eyes and dreamy stance. "We shoulda kept the frigging crib. Now I gotta dish out fifty bucks for a brand-new one."

Lillian looked at him, frustrated by his lack of empathy. Joe earned good money. Cost was not the issue. But she'd decided to get rid of the crib, and any decision other than his own was grounds for upset. Changing the subject to avoid an argument on such an important day, she asked, "Did you come up with a name? I mean, if we get her, we'll need a name."

"No." Joe wheeled the vacuum cleaner towards her.

"Yeah, let's see what happens. The kid might already have a name," Joe countered, eyeing the vacuum cleaner and nodding at the rug.

Lillian understood the menace behind the look. It was a threat. Obey, or else. Dutifully, to avoid another slap, kick, or punch, she cleaned the thick carpet. Pushing and pulling in neat lines until the fibers saluted at a simultaneous angle, the way Joe liked them, her mind was a million miles from the whir of the Electrolux's loud belch as it sucked up a corner of the clown rug. Bending to tug its woolen corner from the beater bar, she beamed at the sunshiny faces of the cartoon clowns. The prospect of a baby gave Lillian a reason to celebrate. The child would slice away the numbing sameness. Going over the disheveled twirl of carpet again, she giggled.

PART II- ARRIVAL

10 Soon-to-be Me

On August 11, 1965, Joe and Lillian Selbach paced the sidewalk outside the Children's Relief Society. An unforgiving sun beat down on the cracked sidewalk. Lillian wiped the perspiration from her top lip. She wanted to wait inside the air-conditioned building, but Joe insisted they wait outside. "We might catch a glimpse of the mother. She might drop the kid off. I wanna see its people. Make sure they're white."

Joe eyed every female pedestrian that passed for signs of urgency. As the minutes eroded, he paced, stopping to check his watch several times. Lillian linked her arm in his, casting his apprehension as the exuberance of an expectant father.

They entered the agency lobby three minutes before their one o'clock appointment. A couple of school-age teens sat in the molded plastic chairs of the waiting room. The young women sat five seats apart, each staring at their folded hands resting in their laps. When one of the women dabbed at her nose with a clenched tissue, the Selbachs exchanged a glance. They wondered if she might be their child's biological mother.

Mrs. Green entered the waiting area in a hurry. "Mr. and Mrs. Selbach. It's lovely to see you. My apologies for the wait. I guess you're ready to see the baby."

"More than ready," soon-to-be mom blurted, following Mrs. Green down the long corridor. Lillian had a habit of speaking out before thinking about or analyzing her words, which planted her marriage and life in an endless spiral of peril.

Two hours earlier, Mrs. Green had carried me down that same hall. She set me in the pretend nursery, a room painted school bus yellow to illicit sunny dispositions in babies and their prospective parents. Under a window overlooking Third Street, the sanitized crib was my fifth stop in the adoption expedition. My first four depots were foster homes where I learned to fear balloons, and everyone called me Janet.

A master of detached happiness, I watched the butterfly mobile twirl above me. My soon-to-be parents stepped into the radiant space, freezing at the sound of my movement.

Lillian held back tears, covering her mouth, "Is that her?"

"Yes," Mrs. Green nudged her towards the crib. "Her biological mother named her Janet. Should she be acceptable, you can, of course, change her name."

Lillian arrived at the crib railing first, leaning over to look at me. "Oh, Joe, look."

Joe joined her at the rail. "She's beautiful."

"She's perfect. May I hold her?" Lillian's eyes filled with tears.

"Of course," Mrs. Green lifted me from the crib, handing me over. I settled into the stranger's arms with the ease of experience. Joe touched my head, pushing a swatch of hair back from my cheek.

"Now. We would like to place the child as soon as possible. So, if she's acceptable, we'd like to complete the rest of the paperwork today."

"You mean we can take her home today?" Lillian asked, inhaling my powdered, baby scent.

I closed my eyes.

"Yes. If you want, I mean, there's no pressure to take this baby."

"We'll take her," Joe announced, pleased with my Germanic blonde hair and deep brown eyes.

"Oh, yes. She will be our Vicki-lynn." Lillian announced, changing my given name in a mystifying instant. I squirmed at the volume of the proclamation.

"Would you like to put her down, so we can tend to the details?" Mrs. Green gestured toward the crib.

"Our baby, Joe. Ours!" Lillian kissed my forehead.

"It's best if you leave her. Please follow me," Mrs. Green replied.

They left me there in the glare of hope. In a baby corral where a hundred other babies had awaited their dispensed fate, I awaited mine.

I later learned that my soon-to-be parents went to Mrs. Green's office next. There, they sat at her desk, watching her add forms to my thick case file. That's when Joe, still curious about my lineage, asked about my parents, "What can you tell us about them?"

"The child's mother is Canadian. She is not married and does not have the financial means to care for the baby. The father was a short-term relationship, and he doesn't know about the child. The mother felt this was better. She wanted the girl to have a mother and father." Mrs. Green looked at the file, "There are very few details here."

"What if she changes her mind?" Joe asked as Lillian signed the five-hundred-dollar check to pay for my adoption.

"She has relinquished all rights to the child. She signed the paperwork, allowing us to place the child in a suitable home."

"So, she can't take her back, no matter what?" Lillian asked. Ownership had begun to fill her mothering cup, and she needed to be sure I was hers. Wary of loving another hopeful thing that she would lose, she held her breath, awaiting the answer.

"No, this is final. It's the law," said Mrs. Green sliding the check into the file and closing it. One flip of her wrist sealed the file for life.

Along with my heritage, medical records, genealogy, and original birth certificate, Janet disappeared. Rearranged, reassigned, and renamed, I became Vicki-lynn Selbach.

"Well, it seems congratulations are in order. Here's your paperwork. We'll mail you an amended birth certificate. It may take some time. The agency is a bit backlogged. So many babies to place."

"That's it? We can take her home?" my new Mommy asked, still questioning her good fortune.

Returning to the baby observatory, they peered at me through the bars, and I watched them from the sleepy tranquility of in-between belonging and being. Even as they transferred me to new Daddy's hard shoulder, I remained complacent and quiet, the way I'd learned to be.

New Mommy carried a small bag filled with two bottles of formula and a few diapers as she walked through the empty lobby. They were all of my possessions besides the yellow romper I wore.

"We gotta get baby crap," new Daddy announced once we arrived at the car. His voice was sharp and oppressive. Clutching me to his shoulder with one hand, he opened the car door with the other. He handed me to the new Mommy in the passenger seat.

The closing of the car door startled me, and I sat in my new Mommy's lap, watching a world of colors pass. I liked car rides and giggled at passing drivers. New Mommy's pale cheeks turned pink as I wiggled my hands in the car window. I didn't know these strangers were my final family or that my forever home would dent the armor I'd worn since birth. I was happy to be moving, leaving someplace old in the warm embrace of someone new.

"Look, Joe, she's waving at the truck driver."

Our first stop after the agency was the furniture department at Stern's department store.

"Can we get the crib today?" new Daddy asked the clerk, who nodded at me, contorting his face playfully and sticking out his tongue.

"Cute, can we move dis along?" new Daddy's eyes narrowed, angry with the plaid-suited salesmen.

"Sure. We'll make sure it's there by six. Wouldn't want this little one to lose a wink of precious sleep," the salesmen winked.

"It better be," new Daddy warned before following new Mommy and me to the clothing department.

We arrived at the cashier with five pink dresses and a double ruffle white bonnet. The gray-haired clerk held my hand as new Mommy wrote a check. She accidentally signed on the *Pay to* line, giggling at the error.

'Sorry," she apologized to the clerk, who shrugged.

"Take your time; she's a cutie."

Tearing up the first check and tucking it at the back of the checkbook, new Mommy wrote a new one. New Daddy tapped his hand on the counter as he waited. The store clerk wrapped each garment in tissue before tucking them into the shopping bag. Unable to wait a minute longer, he lifted me from the counter.

"Hurry up," new Daddy ordered. "I'd like to get the kid home this year." The tension in his grip was familiar, like all the hands that had touched me before. It is impossible to carry a stray without some rigid recognition of their hardship.

New Mommy explained away her husband's behavior. "We adopted her today. She's our first, and it's all a bit overwhelming."

The clerk frowned as new Daddy stomped towards the exit. "Congratulations. It looks like you're going to have your hands full," he said, shaking his head.

New Mommy lifted the bag, running to catch up. I watched over new Daddy's shoulder as the exit door closed in her face.

11 Noel

I recall my first year as a Selbach in photographs and the telling and retelling of stories. I think it was happy. I loved my parents. Yet, I'm sure I missed the first mother. Her absence, a river that flowed beneath every childhood experience, was not wholly dark, for it was also security, a silent understanding that there was a before and might be an after.

As an infant, the misplacement of the first mother had not ripened to understanding. Only for the first month did I wake up every morning screaming. Then, with my physical needs well met, I smiled a lot. I appeared content in my new life as Vicki-lynn. The infant named *Janet* fell away amid celebrations and life firsts.

I recall my mother's family in great bold sounds and aromatic food aromas. Like a safe, bubbly, pink cluster of balloons that never popped unexpectedly, they were the relatives who taught me to talk with my hands, speak my mind, and eat well. The Italians gave me my sparkle.

~ ~ ~

Motherly enthusiasm, diapers, and a refreshed sense of purpose filled the months leading up to my first birthday. Christmas festivities took on a revived sparkle for my mother. She arranged birthday and Christmas gifts under the blue-lit Christmas tree. My presents, wrapped in the prettiest pink wrap Mommy could find at Woolworths, stood out among the green and red holiday packages.

Christmas Eve 1965 was the coldest the city of New York had seen in ten years. Daddy arrived from a half day of work, clapping his hands and booming, "Where's my girl?"

With the breeze that clung to his wool coat, Daddy carried a white cake box tied with red baker's string. Putting down the cake before removing his jacket, he stole down the hall to my room. Mommy watched him approach my crib, heartened by his soft countenance. Since my arrival, coddling and spoiling had replaced Daddy's after-work brooding.

I opened my eyes at the sound of their approach. Anguish did not yet cloak my parent's existence. Mommy scooped me into her arms to follow Daddy to the Christmas tree. Bending on one knee, Daddy removed the pink presents one at a time. "Lillian, I want her to think her birthday's important. I don't want her birthday mixed with all that holiday crap. Your family knows it's a birthday party, right?"

"Of course. My family may bring Christmas gifts, but she'll know it's her birthday." Mommy swayed, holding me on her hip.

She put me in my wooden playpen. I watched through the slats as she added hard candy to a crystal dish on the stereo console, humming the "Happy Birthday" tune. Stashes of mints, ribbon candy, and hard candy treats dotted the living room. Garland streams and tinsel decorated every wall. Our home wore the happiness of the holiday like a crown.

"Frigging guineas better not screw this up. You get one first birthday. I got the cake from that German bakery by my parent's place. So much better than that wop crap you got for my birthday." Daddy was nice sometimes. But even when he was delivering what he thought was a compliment, condemnation iced the words with criticism.

Mommy ignored him, retreating to the kitchen to skin the fish and peel shrimp for the Sicilian Feast of the Seven Fishes. The meal was a Christmas Eve tradition named for the seven sacraments of the Roman Catholic Church and required hours of preparation.

Daddy freed me from the playpen, propping me up on the long, tufted couch as guests arrived. I clung to his powerful arms, content to be close to him as he let go. Like a golden trophy, I was Daddy's favorite thing. He looked at me with a sparkle in his blue eyes, and I beamed.

The quiet moment with Daddy faded as my Papa and Mama and Mommy's sisters Helen and Rose arrived. Tapping on the front door, they let themselves in. "We're here," Mama announced as the group entered in a rush of conversation. As was always the case when Mommy's family visited, the room took on a celebratory aura. Chairs dragged to the living room supplied plenty of seating. Gertz Department Store bags stuffed with wrapped goodies surrounded the tree.

Cheers flowed as family members raised glasses of Sambuca. "To Christmas and family," Papa said before downing the clear liquor.

Lively conversations ebbed and flowed as my family nibbled on the array of appetizers set on TV trays around the room. There was eggplant caponata, prosciutto-wrapped provolone, and marinated mushrooms. As plates emptied, the family turned their focus to me. Their ticklish kisses and enthusiastic expressions made me giggle.

Daddy pulled at one end of the expandable table, and Papa took the other side. They opened it and added the leaf stored aside the fridge for occasions when we needed more space. In the kitchen, my Mama helped with the final touches of the multi-course meal. "Stir the marsala, Lillian; the mushrooms will burn."

Armloads of food arrived next, and Mommy moved me to my highchair. "Heavenly Father," my Papa started the prayer of thanks, and everyone bowed their heads. All eyes closed or stared engorged with reverence, except Daddy's and mine. He made funny faces at me, ignoring the seriousness of the Barbiera family's worship. I banged my feet on the foot rail of the chair, giddy with the attention.

"Amen." Papa eyed Daddy, who ignored him.

As soon as he lowered his clenched hands, a great wash of tangled arm reaching and fork stabbing ensued. My family feasted on baked clams, spaghetti with mussels, and shrimp marsala. Papa Rosario filled wine glasses from the Chianti jug that rested at his feet. "Mangia, Mangia," he toasted.

My family ate until waistbands strained and lips smacked satisfied. I looked on, pinching Cheerios and giggling at my Papa's elastic expressions.

After dinner, Daddy placed my birthday cake on the wooden tray of my chair. It was a creamy Bavarian-centered masterpiece with piped pink roses. Camera bulbs flashed, startling me for a moment. Papa blew on a paper party horn, and Mama pinched my cheeks, praising the cake. "Almost as pretty as you, Vicki-lynn," she cooed.

Daddy watched as the flashbulbs lit the brown of my eyes. I wore the pin-tucked bib dress he had chosen. It was one of a half-dozen stunning ensembles he'd purchased for me at Gimbals. Over-indulgence defined the early days of our father-daughter relationship. My arrival established a new pecking order in our home. Mommy faded into a sideshow in Daddy's circus as I became his main attraction.

Daddy left the room as soon as the buttercream masterpiece was in front of me. I examined the puffy white confection, wondering if I should touch it. My relative's eyes widened when Daddy returned carrying a life-size teddy bear, and I looked away from the cake to the stitched-on face of the bright pink bear. Daddy sat the toy on a dining chair next to me, and picture-taking resumed.

"You'll spoil her, Joe," Mommy teased, swatting Daddy's arm playfully.

Mommy lit the pink candles. The glow reflected off my white-blonde hair. As I inspected my rapt audience, Daddy took my hand. Wiping it against the smooth icing, he put my fingers to my lips. My mouth exploded with happiness at the sugary surprise.

Daddy backed up, grinning and nodding. I reached forward, coating both hands in the gooey confection. Eating fistfuls of frosting, I squealed with delight. It was a sentimental moment, ripe with love for my father.

It would be one of the last.

Soon, the man I called Daddy would burn away amid the acidic corrosion of fear and leave my heart to ache for the slant-grinned, dimple-cheeked man who loved me.

12 Skyscrapers

Giggles are a commodity in the world of daughters and fathers. My first memory of Daddy making me laugh was a peek-a-boo session. He peeked around the corner of my room as I stood in my crib, waiting for whatever would come after my nap. I immediately spotted his playful grin and the waving of his hands as he said, "Peek a boo. I see you," in a sing-song voice. He ducked behind the closet door, and I waited for him to reappear. When he did, he said, "Boo," and I cracked up. Lifting my arms to him, I recall the joyful expectation of his embrace. A quick spin after I was in his arms thrilled me again, and I belly-laughed the way only toddlers can.

My father was not always toxic. Once upon a time, I looked up to him. I saw him as I believe fortunate daughters see their Dads with great big arms and beaming confidence. On that peek-a-boo day, he tossed my giggling form into the air, and I knew he would catch me. I continued to know he would catch me until he did not.

This was the day I learned to fear Joe Selbach.

~ ~ ~

When I was a small child, I thought my father was brave for his ability to walk on air. I shut my eyes now, trying to recall my first memory of his sky walking. I see Daddy at work, twenty-two stories above Brooklyn, with the city's mud-caked waterway to the right and a clear view of Battery Park on the left.

There, he and five other ironworkers dangled their legs as Mommy and I waited beside the car, each shielding our eyes from the sun. Finally, a whistle sounded from atop the site office. The men grabbed their black metal lunch boxes. Walking single file on a narrow beam, they exited the scaffold. Taking turns, two at a time, they descended into the construction elevator.

When Daddy came into view, I waved frantically, craving his attention. He waved back, stopping to talk with a few of his co-workers. The men spoke loud enough for me to hear bits and pieces of the conversation.

"I tell you what," Daddy shouted, "three new injuns today. You hear that Red bragging on how he worked Verrazano without a wire? How many times we done that? Shithead stared at me all superior, insinuating they're some kinda gifted climbers. Shit, buddy, tell me about it when you got your first high-rise scalping by TWA."

"Yeah, Selbach, that job was sometin. I know a coupla guys who might still be kicking if you and your Dad hadn't worked that bridge."

Daddy gloated, raising his palm to high-five his friend Scottie who'd been to our house a lot. "Never got me an injun, though," Daddy shrugged, and the men laughed.

"Dey ain't crap," a ruddy-faced redhead chimed, his mouth puckered around a cigarette as he spoke. "Next thing you know, we'll be working with monkeys." The man wiped the grit of a hard day's work from his face with his shirt sleeve.

Stretching an arm behind him, my Daddy shook his head. "Not on my watch. I rather eat shit than work with a nigger."

I did not blink nor grimace at the racial slur. The term, used so often in my childhood home, did not yet carry the burden of its foul history. In the language of my family's dysfunction, I learned the word to be an appropriate description of dark-skinned people.

A breeze whipped from the east, and the other man standing with my father commented, "Cold's coming. That'll scare off half of them injuns."

Daddy looked our way, opened his lunchbox, and took the last swig of the Schlitz my mother had packed frozen at four a.m. Eight hours under the open sky had melted the amber liquid cool and palatable.

"Night," Daddy nodded to each man. He removed his hard hat to join us for the twenty-minute commute home. The smell of burnt metal and perspiration accompanied us as we rode silently. Then Daddy turned on the radio, switching stations from FM easy-listening music to AM news.

The newscaster's words meant nothing to me but elicited a deep grumble from my father. "Military police used clubs today to repulse anti-war demonstrators outside the Pentagon. Several protesters slipped through the MP lines and entered the building."

"Fucking hippies. Who do they think they are? I did my time. Ought to round up the lot and send 'em over to kill a few gooks. That'll shut their traps," Daddy spit.

"Gook, gook, gook?" I chanted the fun-sounding word from the backseat, kicking my feet against the driver's seat.

"Stop kicking me, you little shit," Daddy yelled in a severe tone that got my attention.

Mommy looked at me in the rearview mirror, holding a finger to her lips and shaking her head. I remained quiet for the rest of the ride.

At home, as I waited for someone to lift me from the back seat, I watched Daddy slap Mommy. It came out of nowhere, a brutal hit to her cheek, which she held as she looked back at me with worried eyes.

Immediately uncomfortable and scared, I cried. Daddy opened the car door, reaching down to lift me, and I pulled back. It was the first fear I'd felt for the man I thought had hung the moon. My eternal love for Daddy grew a thick coat of caution at that moment. I loved him still but understood that his hugging hands could also hurt.

I struggled for a moment, leaning away from him. He waited stone-faced in the opening of the car door for the exhaustion to come. A head-strong child, I had what my parents called temper tantrums. I fell asleep after every fiery display.

Not temper but fear bubbled in my teary display that day. Still, my three-year-old body defied my upset. Worn out, I stopped crying. Daddy scooped me into his arms, and I laid my head on his shoulder. He was still Daddy, and I was still his daughter as he carried me into the apartment. The peril I recognized in Joe Selbach faded in the close tenderness of his embrace.

13 Baby Boy Blue

Saplings growing side-by-side come to rely on their intermingled roots for sustenance. Where one ends, the other begins. They share the rain and the sun in equal measure. This is how my adoptive brother and I grew inseparable.

You cannot wipe the blood from someone's body again and again without it staining your heart. Daddy did not hit me often, and that made Peter's suffering worse. I lived in a glass skeleton, shivering and wishing my father would shatter me in the same way he battered the others. I begged to be hit, for that would have been fair.

What happened to us was never fair. It wasn't even about us.

~ ~ ~

Three tinseled Christmases later, violence swelled in our Flushing home. Mommy and Daddy adopted my brother Peter on August 11, 1968. Like most things experienced once, the second adoption was easier. My parent's application flew through Mrs. Green's eager hands, and my cheerful three-and-a-half-year-old demeanor became a barometer for my parent's suitability. I wish I'd appeared sadder for the sake of my brother, who I love with the depth of a caregiver, confidant, and playmate.

Mommy filled out the application papers, leaving out Daddy's Easter morning attack and how he'd fractured her wrist in two places. She avoided the truth of her bruised limbs and tumbles down stairs for the good of a waiting orphan. Somewhere another child needed her.

Daddy's viciousness quelled after my adoption. Mommy thought the sibling solution might plug his mean streak for good, especially if they got a boy. Mommy believed Daddy might connect with a boy since he'd lost contact with his natural-born son. The boy he had kept secret at the start of their marriage. As so many times before and since, Mommy was mistaken.

They scooped up my mahogany-haired, olive-skinned baby brother from the same crib where they met me. Mommy fell in love immediately. Daddy did not. On the morning of the adoption, I stayed close to him with my best friend, Suzy Silber, and her mother, Shelley.

The Silbers were the Selbachs' closest friends. Daddy had met Ronnie, a larger-than-life man with a booming voice and beautiful intellect, when he'd sold him insurance. Dad and Ronnie hit it off immediately, making weekend plans with families in tow, and lifelong friendships ensued.

The Silber family's presence meant safety, and I held Suzy's hand as we eyed my brother, for whom I was already worried. Suzy's parents were my favorite adults, for they often whisked Mom and me away to happy places and fun. When Aunt Shelley's little yellow Volkswagen pulled into the Selbachs' drive, it was always a sign of better times.

All eyes were on the baby boy who would become my brother. But I watched Daddy. When the others moved towards the crib, he stepped back. Tilting his head as if inspecting a mosquito he'd like to squash, Daddy looked at the baby boy as if he had disappointed him in some undefinable way.

Mommy and Shelley chatted about my brother's long eyelashes. Suzy squeezed my hand, excited to be sharing in the arrival of my sibling. No one else seemed to notice Daddy's agitated reaction. I tried to take Daddy's hand, but he pulled away. I had learned to be cautious when my father's mood fouled, but I could not help but love him. My brother whimpered. Daddy looked at me, wearing an expression of loathing that tilted the axis of my childhood.

We took the baby boy home, and our apartment seemed to shrink with his arrival. Mommy and Daddy started to talk about buying a house. He became Peter Allen Selbach. They named him for Mommy's grandfather, a descendant of Ethan Allen. Allen fought against Great Britain during the American Revolution. He became famous for leading the Green Mountain Boys to capture Fort Ticonderoga.

No matter what we called him, Peter was a fussy five-month-old who grew crankier by the week. Only constant human touch quelled his needy howling. I often held my baby brother in my lap, rocking him to erase his panicked look of displacement. I grew older then. Casting away the last innocence of a carefree childhood, I became my brother's protector.

Stepping between my father's unfathomable fury and my baby brother was a dangerous choice. It scared me but somehow felt natural, practically predestined. The frivolity of youth was a privilege I would not visit again. Unceasing faith and an unbreakable sibling bond would be my eventual reward.

Peter's first birthday was in March of 1969. Daddy did not take part in planning his special day, and Mommy chose an iced chocolate cake from her favorite Italian bakery.

Standing at the yellowed countertop, she pressed blue candles into piped blue roses. Admiring her handiwork, she winced when Daddy slammed the door. Dropping his lunch box with a loud clatter, he looked at the cake and grunted, "What's this crap?"

Mommy hurried to stir the chicken soup bubbling on the stove. "It's Peter's cake."

"No one's coming. So why do we need a cake? He'll blubber all over the damn thing. He's had that cold for a week."

Grabbing a beer, Daddy pounded past our bedroom. We looked up from our play until he disappeared into the living room. I retrieved a Matchbox car from under my brother's crib. Every weekday after breakfast, I hid my brother's favorite toy there. It was the perfect surprise to keep him from crying when Daddy got home.

With one hand on the toy, I watched Daddy pass again, headed to the shower. Most days, Daddy scowled past us in a hurry to rinse away the reek of hard work in the city. Peter usually cried at the sight of him, conditioned to expect something awful.

Daddy stopped in the hall, observing us with a faraway look. For a hopeful moment, I dropped the toy, thinking he might remember that he loved us. I smiled at him, remembering the day he pushed me on the park swing, and how he laughed as I slid down the metal slide face-first. I had re-enacted the trick repeatedly, relishing his rare expression of joy.

Daddy turned to walk away from our doorway. I diverted my brother's attention, rolling the car across the floor. "Vroom," Peter giggled at the driving sounds I imitated. Toddling towards the toy, he tripped, attempting to catch it. His lip puffed outward, warning of an explosion.

I tossed the car in the air, "Boom," I exclaimed, tickling his tummy to dissuade him from crying. Daddy did not like crying, and he also hated burnt toast, blabbering about soap operas, and sloppy towels in the bathroom. Punishment for such transgressions was big-handed hurt.

A few minutes later, the sound of the television reached us. Done with his shower, Daddy settled in for the broadcast. I laid back on the floor, listening.

The reporter announced, "Apollo 9 splashed down in the Atlantic today after a ten-day orbit of Earth. The crew landed within three miles of the recovery ship about 341 miles north of Puerto Rico."

The smell of soup wafted in. Peter stopped fussing. Taking the corner of my blanket, I wiped his runny nose.

Mommy gathered us for dinner before calling Daddy to eat. I placed the thick phone book on my seat, reaching up to help Mommy lock the tray of Peter's highchair. Immediately unhappy at his entrapment, my brother's brow scrunched to a hysteric squint. His lower lip quivered. I hurried to jingle the bell of the suction cup soldier attached to the tray. Uninterested in the toy, he began to cry. I made faces, trying to distract him.

Mommy removed the soup from the stove. It was the same Spicy Sicilian Soup my Papa had eaten as a child. Mommy wondered what her father would think of her sweet interpretation of his favorite family recipe. "Good chili, good health," he'd said every time they ate it. She had left out the chilies to make it easier on her American children's palates.

Straining a small cup of broth for Peter, who could not chew the bite-sized chunks of chicken, Mommy blew on a piece of carrot to cool it. She turned just as Daddy's open palm hit the back of Peter's head. His one-year-old neck snapped forward, stunning him into silence. What had started as a cry of entrapment grew into a wailing state of torture.

Daddy marched toward Mommy, who froze motionless, holding the cup of soup out from her body in a beggar's stance. I watched from the faraway place my mind went whenever Daddy raged. A God-given safety net, I reacted to terror by blanking my mind and acting as if I was larger than Daddy.

"Fucking soup, that's what you make a man for dinner? I bet those Apollo show-offs had better meals in that goddamned tin can." Pointing at Peter, he continued, "Can't you shut your fucking kid up?"

I slid forward on the telephone book until my toes touched the floor. All the while holding onto the only part of Peter I could reach. I tried to still the balled-up fist he banged incessantly on the wood tray.

As my feet reached the floor, an unexpected soup shower sprayed over us. I rubbed Peter's hands as I peered over his shoulder, licking the salty splatter from my lips. Rage churned in Daddy's eyes as he held the now empty soup pot over the place where Mom had been cooking. Mom shrieked and, zigzagging from the room, grasped her soaked side.

I stared at the rainbow of vegetables on the floor. The slow tremble of shock that always accompanied surprise attacks crawled up my back. I called it the melt, for the bubbling melt of skin I was sure slid from my brow to my chin.

I had named the feeling of mental separation *the melt* after spotting an abandoned baby doll on the porch of a burned city dwelling. Soot-covered, the doll resembled the half-melted candle mom kept in the junk drawer in case of a power outage. The puckered and bubbled doll became a visual representation of my terror.

Peter wailed. Writhing to escape the warm liquid puddled on his tray, he sopped my already moist shirt as he splashed. Tremors wracked my shoulder blades, working their way down to wobble my knees. I clasped my hands over my ears, trying to quash the bellowing that swept over the room in a mad gallop. The house was a cave of echoing misery.

I looked at the chaos of my parent's battle, then back at my brother, and springing into action, I took a towel from the oven door. I sopped up as much of the oily liquid as I could manage. The highchair tray glistened with broth and dead white chunks of chicken. Moving the step stool to the sink, I wrung it out, returning to collect the rest of the boiling soup.

Struggling with the latched tray, I tried to release my brother from his wet misery. As soon as my tiny, uncoordinated fingers had one side unclasped, Peter pounded his fists, re-clicking the tray. I was on my third attempt when I heard the slam of salvation. The crash of the apartment door sent the soup spoon, which hung precariously at the edge of the table, to the floor in a quiet splash.

Daddy left Mommy in the bathroom, hanging over the sink with her arm submerged in cold water. The hot soup had landed on her right arm, which was beet red and beginning to blister. After smacking the back of her head with a wallop that careened her head into the mirror, Daddy marched past us, stopping to survey the scene. He wore a grandiose expression that made me feel we were part of a morbid test. Daddy looked that way a lot after hurting us, and I often wondered if he did it to see how we'd react.

Daddy did not free his blubbering son from the soupy mess that I was trying to fix. He exited the chaotic scene in the same manner he had created it, without an iota of regret.

The air in the apartment grew lighter with Daddy's departure. I leaned all my weight on the silver latch of the highchair, finally managing the simultaneous switch that freed my brother. Peter slid from the highchair, an escaped squid slipping and flailing. As I caught his chicken-fat covered body, we fell to the wax-stained linoleum. Rocking my baby brother, I let go of the deep breath I had held until he was safe.

As soon as Mommy's pain eased to mobile tolerance, she found her way back to us. Sinking to the floor, she held us with her unblemished arm. We clutched each other in the glistening puddle, weeping. Our agony became a collective groan that I was sure God could hear in heaven. I prayed silently, "God, please stop my Mommy's arm from hurting and make Daddy nice again."

We remained in the huddle until none of us could produce another tear. Cemented in a solidarity of unescapable want, we would soldier on against the enemy who I still needed to love.

Peter's cake sat atop the counter, uneaten until the following morning. Mommy lit a candle, we sang happy birthday, and we ate the cake for breakfast.

14 Medford

Over the cobblestone path, up the front stoop, through the metal storm door, past the attic stairs and the corner where Daddy's green chair sits. Turn right to the bedrooms where you barricade yourself in, left to the kitchen and den where boiling water is a weapon and Daddy punches fist marks in the plaster walls over and over.

I cannot erase the wood floors and brown appliances of my most trying residence. I close my eyes and walk the halls often; the electric fear of the place is so momentous that it raises the hair on my arms, even in memory.

The fear, loathing, and desperation that lived in that three-bedroom dwelling haunt my dreams. But the Medford house did not start that way. It was once a magical place where deliverance was possible.

~ ~ ~

Men in flannel shirts hammered thick wooden posts, their boots sinking in layers of long dead leaves and dry pine needles. The sound of tapping filled the dense woods that covered the property. Dad hired the surveyors to mark the boundary of his purchased parcel. He hoped to plant fast-growing Cyprus along the border to keep nosy neighbors at bay. For now, long lines of fluorescent twine sufficed.

We watched the men carry and work the boards into the soil. To us, the acre of woods stretched on forever, providing innumerable hiding places. Tall oaks shaded the concrete foundation of our new home, offering protection and hope.

Dad had argued against the purchase for months. "You nuts? We can't afford a new house, Lillian. The way you spend my frigging money, we're lucky we got dis dump."

In Suffolk County, one hour north of the clam-rich waters of the Great South Bay, the town of Medford was ripe with suburban sprawl. Like Levittown in the 1950s, families abandoned city life in droves. At $40,000 for a three-bedroom ranch with a full basement and attic, the property seemed like a pipe dream to Dad, who spewed out questions that Mom disregarded. "My commute ain't long enough? Who's gonna mow all that crap anyhow?"

Mom had grown accustomed to Dad's grumbling disagreement. She visited the bank alone, securing a mortgage to quell his arguments. Her brave actions were born of a need to move from the Deer Park neighborhood where Peter had presented her with a fat, dead rat. "Look, Mommy, kitty," he'd blurted.

Mom swatted the rotting cat-sized creature from his hands. It was the first of several four-legged vermin discovered under the weeping willow of our front yard, and the neighborhood teemed with a two-legged variety as well. The crime was up, and she wanted out.

I followed Peter into the brush of our unfamiliar yard. The crackle of leaves underfoot assured that he would not get far from my watchful eye. Smiling at the dappled light of the tree canopy, I announced, "Fairies live here."

Peter shrugged his shoulders, looking at me like I was daft, then took off in a run. Watching my brother scissor his way past the thick trees, I imagined gnomes and princesses waiting for us. I twirled. My open eyes were mesmerized by the magical forest that sparkled under clouds of glistening rainbow dots. Dreaming while awake is useful when your parents are always making dangerous mistakes.

When the sound of Peter's trot faded from earshot, I returned to reality, where my brother always needed saving. Taking off after him, I hurdled over fallen limbs, panicked by his disappearance. Catching up as he grabbed the bottom branch of a tall oak, I examined its climbability. Its multi-layered branches spread out like a ladder. Helping Peter up the first branch, I followed close behind.

We sat, holding hands, each dreaming a different version of the same story. My mind danced with a fairy trio, flying us off to a faraway knoll. Mom's voice interrupted from beyond the tree line, "Lunch."

I held my brother's foot securely on each branch as he followed me down the gnarled gray bark of the tree. "Maybe Dad will build us a fort here," I said, hopeful. Peter shrugged again, racing past me to the concrete foundation-turned-picnic area.

Mom sat on a plaid blanket spread across the cold cement. Smoothing it, she waved as we emerged from the back tree line. We rushed to the picnic spot, where crouching Indian style, we accepted bologna and cheese sandwiches. We washed the sandwiches down with red Kool-Aid poured into the collapsible drink cups Mom stored in her purse.

Dad approached, and we froze. Like a movie monster surveying a city he'd soon terrorize, he pointed at the symmetrical orange lines marking his land. "That's some yard. Huh, kids?" We exhaled simultaneously.

Visits to the site became a weekend ritual. The packed picnic basket and a twenty-five-minute drive to Route 112 transformed our little family. White hot fear curled away like smoke extinguished by the significant blow of wishing for better days.

At the sound of a truck pulling up, Mom stopped gathering the Wonder Bread crusts Peter had peeled from his sandwich. The driver approached our picnic, dropping the cigarette he'd been smoking in the dirt of the lot. Without bothering to squash the butt, he sidestepped a two-by-four to reach Dad. Thinking his shoes were far too dressy for a Saturday romp through the muck of the construction site, I watched Dad's cheek for the twitch that always preceded an outburst.

Dad folded the blueprints in a hurry and slid them under the picnic basket. The plans showed a finished basement, a feature added after the tax assessment was complete.

"Stay here," he ordered as Peter peeled the last end from his sandwich. I snacked on dreams of my soon-to-be-built pink room and a pudding pack. I was not interested in going anywhere.

Dad met the man with the plaid pants and balding head before he could step onto the plywood that would eventually be our first floor. The man looked at his now dirty shoes and Dad's boots before extending a hand.

"Hi, neighbor. I'm just down the block. Ours was the fifth house built in here. Looks like things are coming along. How long 'til you move in?"

Daddy shook the man's hand roughly, squeezing.

"Whoa there," the neighbor protested, flexing his squashed hand before pulling another cigarette from the pack stowed in his shirt pocket. 'So, what's da name?"

Dad swatted at the noxious smoke, stepping sideways to avoid inhalation. "Selbach, Joe Selbach," He extended his hand to Jean as Mom poured second helpings of Kool-Aid from the Tupperware pitcher.

Jean took his hand warmly and asked, "What's your line? I'm an AA man myself. American Airlines. Names Jean Miller." He took a long drag on the Pall Mall, eying the landscape spikes that marked the perimeter.

"Ironworker, Local 361," Dad replied. "You got an acre?"

"Nah, just the lots on this side of Olympia have that much. Sliced out a quarter on my end."

Pleased at possessing more land than his neighbor, Dad spoke softer. "Yeah, kids are happy, lots of trees for hiding. They beg to come out here with me every weekend."

Peter and I exchanged a knowing glance at the many situations that might force us into hiding and how we would never beg to do anything with Dad. Mom stood to join the men.

"Hide and seek. Sure. My kid, Jimmy, might like to join 'em. He's got the energy to burn."

Dad introduced Mom, "Nutso meet neighbor," he said, smirking.

"I'm Lillian," she corrected.

"Jean. My wife's Chung. From Korea. You two'll have to meet."

"Sure," Mom watched Dad's expression. She appeared curious, wondering if Dad would dismiss the man now that he'd admitted to being married to a foreigner.

"Little mail order momento?" Dad asked.

"Ha-ha, you're funny, Seebake, was it?"

"Selbach," Dad answered, glancing blankly in our direction. We sat waiting for Mom to excuse us from the blanket.

"Gotta get back to lunch before the wolves eat it," Dad remarked, pointing at us.

"Sure, sure," Jean agreed. "Stop by when you get settled." Before Jean could turn to leave, a county cop car pulled up, its bumper close to touching Jean's truck.

"Don't look now, but you're getting a ticket." Dad nodded toward the cop.

"Harassing the new guy already?" the cop asked, emerging from the cruiser like a too-long straw popping from a kiddie cup. Wearing a broad grin, he offered, "Sorry he got to you first. We're not all corrupt 'round here."

The cop removed his cap, running a hand through his thick brown mane before offering it to Dad, "Names Greg Deetham. Welcome to the neighborhood."

Mom gushed, "I'm Lillian." Greg Deetham had sitcom good looks and towered a hand taller than our father.

Dad blocked Mom's extended hand. "Joe Selbach, City Ironworker."

You mean you're one of them acrobats that climb the bridges?" Greg shook his head, "Not me, no way. I'd take a rotten crook over that any day; hate heights."

"Really, from where I'm standing, yew got that covered beanpole," Jean chided.

"We can't all be lawn jockeys," Greg answered, slapping him on the shoulder.

"Gotta run. Lunch. I'll keep an eye on the place 'til you get moved in," the cop assured.

Greg studied him and winked. "See ya when yew gets back. Later, Jean. Kiss your wife for me."

"You wish, Deetham," Jean answered, turning to leave as well.

"Nice guys, especially da cop," Dad said before biting into his waiting salami sandwich. Mom nodded, recalling when she found out Dad was not a police officer.

"Can we be excused?" Peter piped.

"Yes. Go." Dad said, picking seed from his front teeth.

We ran back to the woods, leaving our parents behind to discuss whatever parents talked about when they were not fighting.

15 Dandelion Dreams

Wishing on a lit candle before the flame singes the sweet foundation is easy. We trust that there's plenty of time to make it so. As a child, I wished on pennies, dandelion breezes, candles, and on my knees in prayer. Surely, there was time for someone in the world to save us.

I often spoke my melody of wishes and prayers in a kind of conversation with the first mother. I called her *Lovey*, and in the breathy voice I always used when speaking forbidden words, I asked her and God to kill my father. I could not see her. I could not see God. They shared the distinct ability to be invisible and present at the same time. I trusted them with my secret hopes.

Imagination flowed in the moments after a wish. In my mind, I created a fantasy life with my real family. In white limousines—the fanciest ride I could imagine—they swooped in to save me from Dad, whisking me, Peter, and Mommy to my rightful home in the palace of a mild-mannered king.

I wish you were here, Lovey.

I wish Daddy would die, God.

Some wishes are better left ungranted.

~ ~ ~

Two seasons of fertilizer, watering, and mowing turned our front yard green. Dandelions swayed, at the end of their season, spreading feathery, white pods on the voluptuous summer breeze. Peter and I lay on a white sheet fresh from the laundry for a sibling picnic.

We daydreamed on our backs with crusts of peanut butter and jelly sandwiches on thin paper plates at our feet. "See that bird, Peter?" I asked, pointing at movement high in the afternoon sky. "It's gonna fly to the sun and back, with a rainbow on its tail all stretched out for us to climb. We're gonna climb all the way to the sun."

"Won't we burn?" Peter asked, shielding his eyes to watch the bird dip and rise on the wind.

"Nope. We'll fly anywhere we want, anytime we want."

"Where we gonna go?" he asked, squinting.

"New York City," I answered, daydreaming the idea I'd perfected in a hundred dreams. "Before we climb the rainbow, we'll get ready. I'll build us a tree house with Daddy's scrap wood. It'll have windows and sweet-smelling straw for us to sleep on."

"I want my bed." Peter leaned to pick one of the dandelions we called powder wishes.

"Our straw will be the comfiest bed ever. Not like our lumpy old mattresses."

I propped myself on one elbow to watch Peter twirl the powder wish. "Before we visit the sun, we'll take our house to the city, hang it up at the prettiest park, high up so no one can get us. Then we'll climb the colors and get our wings."

"I'm jumping on blue. Do rainbows have blue?" Peter's brown eyes sparkled.

"Sure, it'll have every color. Once we get our wings, we'll fly out of here. We'll go to our happy place and stay forever. People will feed us and watch us through binoculars. We'll wash in puddles and play on the playground. If anyone scares us, we'll fly to our little building. Gonna be fun, huh?"

"What about Mommy? Will Mommy come?" Peter looked concerned.

"I'm not sure," I answered, wanting to bring my mother into the dream but fearing her flight would get us chased and caught.

Peter sat up. "I'm not going without Mommy."

I rose to sit crisscross applesauce, grabbing a powder wish in one hand and caressing Peter's tiny palm with the other. "Time for wishes."

"I wish Mommy can come with," Peter proclaimed before blowing on his dandelion to unleash a summer snow of dancing white.

"You better go catch one, or it won't come true." Peter leaped from the blanket to hop and jump at the fleeing wishes.

I lifted my chin to the sun, my face warm and bare feet cozy in the grass. Blowing on my dandelion, I hoped for the guts to make the plan a reality. The dandelion scattered, one feathery seed landing on my shorts for easy capture.

"I didn't get any," Peter complained, returning to the sheet as I caught the wisp of white.

"It's okay. I got mine."

Peter rolled over on his stomach. Digging in the grass, he searched for the place where earthworms hid between rainstorms when they covered the street.

I watched the tiny puffs of promise float toward the sun, praying for my wish to come true. Medford had become a roomier prison for our family. The house had more doorknobs and hard surfaces on which Dad could make us suffer.

That night after sunset, our lazy day wishes vanished as Peter's four-year-old skull melded with the knob of the front door. The force of the impact left a lock-shaped indentation on his forehead.

In the critical hours after dusk, Peter had asked Mom for ice cream a third time. In a poorly timed circumstance, our father entered the room as Mom rebuked, "No, Peter, you had cookies."

"You heard your mother, you little shit." Dad exploded across the linoleum. Before his fist could reach my brother's head, I dodged between them, tripping Dad, who stumbled. Peter rushed down the hall. Dad shoved me aside. It was my turn to falter.

Dad caught Peter, who had run straight for the front door. Swiping at my brother's head with an open hand, Dad missed the first time. Peter bit his lip as Dad balled his hand into a fist. The second swing rammed his tiny forehead into the doorknob.

I hurried down the short hall to help him, falling to the floor to hold him. The blood from his head seeped through my spread fingers. Mom stood at the end of the hallway, staring in panicky incapacity. She watched the blood-splattered scene until my father enacted his habitual post-attack retreat. Dad stomped through the living room to the sliding glass door, slamming it so hard that it rattled the key hanging on the metal railing that led to the attic.

Like a prisoner following an imposed routine, Mom went to the bathroom for a cloth to press against Peter's wound. Gathering her purse and keys, she nudged our spent bodies from the floor.

We left quietly, each enacting a well-rehearsed role. I soothed my brother, keeping the melt at bay. Mom drove, glancing at our slumped huddle in the rearview mirror. Tears streamed down her face. Peter sucked in his lip, crying and writhing as the car rolled towards the familiar blue and white emergency room doors.

"How ya doing, Peter?" the emergency receptionist asked as Mom led us to the stark white light of the waiting area. The receptionist winked at me, and I smiled despite the incessant burn in my stomach, resulting from a childhood ulcer that surprised and baffled my doctor.

"Not many kids get them," he told Mom. "She must have a nerve problem."

By the time the nurse called Mom and Peter into a room, my brother's thick bangs were stuck and bloodied. The nurse peeled strands of hair from his swollen forehead to reveal the deep gash. Examining Peter's tear-stained cheek, the nurse assured, "You'll be okay, kiddo. Got a lollipop for you after we get you all fixed up."

Mom explained away Peter's injury with tales of clumsy episodes. No one questioned her truth.

"Just five stitches, mister cutie," the nurse informed in a worried whisper. She completed the final stitch to close the gaping hole where Dad had scarred Peter's head. Stitched up more times than he'd had birthdays, he cried upon seeing the needle, but never during the actual stitching.

"Here you go, baby," the nurse handed him the promised purple lollipop.

To me, his head looked horrible, the rapidity of the seeping blood more extreme than usual. I prayed silently for my brother to live. Survival was the central theme of my prayers, except when I was praying for God to kill my father. I often wonder what God thought of my conflicted childhood messages.

Wiping at the dried blood on my plaid skirt, I cupped my hands to hide the baseball-size blood stain on my lap. Abuse is embarrassing, and a permanent branding that I once believed cast me lower and less than the rest of the world.

Mom carried my brother, who dozed, exhausted by the miserable episode. "Come on," Mom nodded towards the door. A pair of toddlers in the waiting area ceased a spinning game to stare at Peter's blood-stained shirt and bandaged head.

"Big boo-boo," the little boy informed his sister. They watched our battered trio shuffle out to the parking lot.

It was close to midnight when we pulled into the driveway of our brown-shingled home. Reflecting the streetlight, the front windows peered like unblinking eyes. The residence, a stoic bystander in the Selbach melodrama, bore witness to every scrape, gouge, and maiming delivered under its black roof.

We returned under a starless sky. Darkness streamed from every window. Even the berry-covered junipers oozed a gloomy foreboding. In her panic, my mother had neglected to turn on the porch light. As we parked behind Dad's pickup, passing headlights startled the cavernous gloom. Mom ducked in defense. Peter slept, his head nestled in my lap in the backseat of the red Maverick. Mom sat up straighter, giggling at her jittery response to the passing car. I waited for her to open the back door before inching my brother's limp body into her waiting arms.

Mom fumbled with the key, dropping it. I searched the cement stoop on my hands and knees, finding it next to her foot. Entering the dimly lit hall, Mom stepped backward at the site of Dad slumped deep in his green rocker. Illuminated by light from the hall, I could see his foot tapping and a slow rocking.

Mom slipped down the hall to put Peter to bed. I waited for a minute, observing my father, squinting to be sure he did not have the shotgun. Satisfied he did not, I joined my mother to tuck Peter in.

Peter squirmed, touching the bandage on his head, and whimpering in his sleep. I held his hand until he settled. Mom crossed the hall to wash the blood from her hands, gathering blood-stained towels in a pile on the floor. I heard Dad's footsteps in the hallway.

I listened to the water running in the bathroom, resting with my sleeping brother to comfort myself as much as him. At the sound of my father's approach, I sat bolt upright. Shutting the bedroom door to just a sliver, I watched to see if Mom would be okay.

My father threw open the bathroom door, eyeing Mom and the mess on the floor. "You better clean this shit up. That kid of yours is a bleeder. How many stitches?"

"Five," Mom answered.

"Well, he's gotta be more careful. Maybe you should move that damn rug. Kid coulda killed himself on it. You're always doing dumb shit like that."

"Yes, Joe," she whispered. "I'll move it right away."

Dad must have construed Mom's answer as an agreement that Peter's injury was an accident. I could see his physical stance change and feel the static confidence that came with the ability to control the truth. Dad narrowed his eyes, looking at Peter's door, where he spotted me watching. "What are yew doing out of bed? Get. Now."

"No, Dad. Peter's hurt. I gotta stay." I opened the door three inches, clutching the doorknob to block Dad from entering. Indifferent to my protective efforts, he heaved me from the room, shoving me down the hall with little effort. I slammed my hands into his chest before he closed my bedroom door. I kicked the wall three times, anger and fear fueling my rage.

"You come out, and they're gonna get it," he shouted before opening Peter's door to ensure he was in bed. It was a threat he knew would silence me. I was afraid of my father but feared the pain he could inflict on my family more.

I sat on the floor of my pink room with the white canopy bed; my ear pressed to the door. The melt settled over me, whispering its usual warning of imminent death. I touched my face, checking for the dripping disfigurement. Frozen and alert, I chanted to stay awake, "You sleep, they die. You sleep, they die."

Fear oozed from the freshly plastered walls of 69 Olympia Avenue, penetrating everything and everyone who entered. Relatives rarely visited. Before friends passed our house, they revved up to a brisk walk or run. It was a cursed place, and I begged God that night, and on hundreds like it, to remove us from the terror of being there with the monster.

"God," I whispered, looking up for some reason, hoping he might hear me better, "please save my family. I'm scared. Sometimes, I want to die. Please let him die instead, God. I hate him, and it's a sin, but I can't help it."

With my ear against the door, I listened with all my strength for signs of renewed tumult, fidgeting to stay awake. Bloody puddles had taught me to stay awake, no matter how much I needed rest. Sleep found me anyway, the sandman turning tears into crusty corners for me to wipe away in the morning.

16 Catastrophe

Howling is not heard merely in the ossicles, those tiny vibrating bones of the middle ear, but it is embedded in the cerebrum, burned into nerve endings, and singed upon the palms of the helpless to pulse in memory for a lifetime.

The sound of murder is eternal. Even the ripping out of eardrums could not remove it.

Believing in escape was harder after this.

~ ~ ~

Relaxing in the soft white light of the pristine coffin filled with pink roses and purple lilacs. Not at all nightmarish, the idea of being dead comforted me. Inside the coffin, the air was stagnant, unemotional, still. The dream gave me a much-needed break from the chaos.

I awoke the following day curled on the floor. Fresh from the casket dream, I yawned.

Digging the sleep from my eyes, I sniffed, hoping to catch a whiff of the aromatic flowers that lined the coffin of my dreams. Smelling nothing, I opened my eyes, stretching before hurrying to my brother's room. His bed was empty.

"Peter," I screamed down the hall, half stumbling, half sliding on the wood floor. I found him in the den, comfortably sprawled on the shag rug, oblivious to my panic. He watched Saturday morning cartoons from under unruly bangs and the thick bandage that covered his stitches. Mom was frying eggs and bacon. Spotting me, she smiled, "You slept late—almost eleven. Dad is in the garage. Get dressed, sleepyhead. You got chores."

Before breakfast, I knelt next to Peter to examine his oozy forehead. "Get off me!" he pushed me away.

"Come on. I want to make sure it's okay."

Peter slid a finger halfway up his nose, trying to gross me out.

"Disgusting." I stuck out my tongue. Convinced he would not bleed to death, I let him be.

Peter sat in a masterful stillness he'd perfected after the move to Medford. Prey knows that movement gets you noticed, increasing the possibility of deadly consequences. Peter chose a cloak of immobility whenever possible.

"I'll weed by myself, Mom. Peter should rest," I informed my mother, determined that Dad would lose a Saturday worker for his bad behavior.

Saturday was weed-pulling day, and the cobblestones were our priority. Dad built the driveway walkway with stolen cobbles from a Long Island Railroad building site. No matter the weather or play possibilities, we pulled weeds on Saturdays until the thin seams between the cobbles were bare. "A smidge of green will make you scream," I reminded Peter whenever we cleared the sandy cracks.

On weekdays when Dad worked in the city, we played after school, the predictability of his six p.m. arrival gifting us three hours of playtime before we returned to tip-toeing silence and fear.

For a long time, I feared the uncertainty of weekends for the way they amplified Dad's malice. Without the safety of school, the forty-eight hours between Friday and Monday became a waiting game. We waited for pain and death, trapped by the randomness of our father's rage.

"The weeds can wait," Mom rubbed my shoulders. "You don't have to shovel it in, honey."

"Just want it outta the way." I ate the last slice of crisp bacon before rinsing my dish. Glancing into the den, I worried about Peter's confused expression and whether the pink center of the bandage meant he was bleeding again. He looked back with faraway eyes. I said nothing, unwilling to interrupt whatever kept his mind from focusing on the pain.

The sound of the electric saw masked my exit. My purple bike with the banana seat leaned against the garage door, reminding me that friends Sofia, Laura, Susan, and Greg would race the neighborhood while I tended to the cobblestones.

Picking dirt from under my short fingernails, I sat on the cobbles watching the road for signs of my friends. The whir of the saw ceased, its stillness stiffening my slouched spine. Dad came from the garage with a hand over his eyes, protecting them from the sun. He squinted at me, a sliver of softness entering his ice-blue eyes. It was a softness I came to despise. I wanted him to hate me as much as I hated him, with the same loathing he held for my brother and mother.

Being left out of the physical beatings felt like a betrayal. Besides a few belt beatings—for interfering in my brother's *punishments*—I remained untouched.

Daddy wiped his hands on the stiff fabric of his army green work pants, and the usual grimace returned. "Hey, Dad," I chirped, trying to sound happy.

"Yeah," Dad yelled. "You missed a few at the front." His thick, calloused finger pointed to where the stones met the front lawn. He was about to say something else when he spotted a cat crouched amid the green of his lawn.

"Another fucking cat, pissing on my property. Get in the house," he ordered, streaming invectives as he headed to the garage.

I watched from inside the screen door as he passed, carrying a canvas sack. Flying up the hall, I panicked. Daddy had done horrible things to animals before.

I jaunted to the driveway-facing window in Peter's room.

From there, I observed Dad's determined tread across the driveway. The chubby calico, transfixed by the aroma of an insect or some other feline delicacy, did not look up at first. It appeared innocent, hungry, adoptable.

The cat looked up. It flicked its tail, appearing used to human interaction. Before it could completely rev its purr box, Dad grabbed the animal by the ruff of its neck. It dangled as if waiting to be raised into a cuddle. Instead, my father dropped the furry intruder in the canvas sack.

Even with the window closed, I heard the cat hiss as it twisted inside, trying to escape. It was the same panicked desperation that sounded in my dreams. I remember thinking we had a lot in common; the cat and me.

I watched, frozen in fear of what he might do to the howling creature with the two-tone fur. When Dad disappeared into the side yard, I ran for help.

"Mom, Mom," I shrieked. She sat with her slippered feet over the arm of the brown colonial-print couch. Peter rested on the floor in front of her, his eyes fixed on the television. Accustomed to adjusting the volume for raucous interruptions, Peter crawled instinctively toward the TV. He turned the volume knob past the faded number five. Spiderman sprayed webs across tall buildings. Peter sat back, flicking his wrist back to emulate his favorite superhero.

I positioned myself between my mother and brother to report my father's activities. Spitting the words, "Dad caught a cat in the front yard. It's in a bag. You have to stop him. He's gonna hurt it. Like the others."

Mom craned her neck to see around me, giggling at the high jinks playing out in the cartoon. She waved me away, "I'm sure he's just getting it out of the yard so that it won't pee in the sandbox."

Mom denied my father's real intention to keep Peter from knowing Daddy had killed animals before. In Deer Park, where we owned two German Shepherds that barked whenever a cat passed our yard, my father prowled the neighborhood, plucking unsuspecting felines from private lawns and asphalt lots until he amassed ten felines in a canvas sack. That afternoon, he drowned them in the Carlls River and bragged about it over Shake 'n Bake pork chops that night. "Got ten today. Should have heard those pussies hiss."

I wanted to believe her; despite all the times she had been wrong in the past. My heart still racing, I passed my brother, ruffling his thick hair before opening the heavy sliding glass door. I stepped into the aluminum, screened-in patio that my father had built one month after we arrived in Medford. Outside, a dozen mowers tidied neighbor's yards. My buzzing worry joined the cacophony of greens keepers as I approached the back of the enclosure.

My hands in prayer-ready position, I peered at the back treeline, following my father's monstrous bootprints. His footprints stopped beside a pile of Tonka trucks abandoned after a day of play. There, with his back to me, Dad stood. The cat was still squirming in the bag he held in a raised fist.

Without realizing it, I wept at the prospect of what he would do next. He was in the patch of pruned pine trees closest to our swing set. Beside him stood the rusty barrel he'd deposited in the yard three months prior. He'd threatened to turn it into a table base, but as weeks became months, the drum remained unused. Rainwater filled it to the brim, forcing Dad to empty it weekly for fear of opportunistic mosquitos. Tilting the heavy drum until its contents soaked the sandy earth, he cursed the insects that dared lay eggs in his barrel.

Dad was motionless, holding the bag away from his body. It was the same way he'd held a paper sack of throw-up when I suffered from motion sickness on a family road trip. The cat's hiss morphed into a scream that sounded so human I turned to see if Peter was okay. My heart leaped hopefully when the bag swayed in Dad's hand, opening for a moment. A white paw poked through the gap. Dad slapped the clawing cat's paw back in, holding the top of the sack tighter.

My father appeared to contemplate the same question I whispered under my breath, "What will he do?"

Dad looked at me, then back at the barrel. As slowly as dragging a knife across a movie victim's throat, he lowered the bag into the waist-high barrel. Every hair on my arms stood up. My breathing stopped. The melt began. Immobilized in a tactile moment between life and death, my diamond-sized tears morphed into a cascade. "Oh no, no, Daddy, no."

I covered my mouth, too afraid to rescue the animal. My breath staggered when I realized I had bellowed. The sound fanned the horror of Dad's cruel immersion. Undaunted by my scream, my father waded in the overflow that sloshed from the barrel. The animal's weight pushed water over the edges changing his work boots from tan to mustard. I dropped my praying hands to my stomach. My ulcer burned into anxious action.

I doubled over, unable to look away. Hope held my eyes steady. It was the same hope that surfaced every time my father performed an unfathomable act. Hope had no business in the cat's drowning death, but I prayed regardless. "Please, God, let it get out. Let it live."

Distracted by the worry of leaving the sliding glass door open, I looked back to find it closed. I turned back to the gruesomeness, assured that the sound of murder would not reach Peter's ears. The water in the barrel undulated less and less. My father lifted the dripping bag, poking at the canvas to see if the intruder was dead. The sound that rose at his jab was the unearthly song of a million demons.

I gagged. The final caterwaul of the half-drowned animal made its way to Mom and Peter, who had just switched off the television. Peter crawled to turn the TV back on. The syncopated beat of the Batman theme song joined the gurgling end of the animal's being.

Mom slid open the door, stepped to the coolness of the cement, and closed the door behind her. I crouched on my knees at the back-screen wall. Mom looked towards the barrel where Dad put the deadly finishing touches on the brutal act. Mom pulled me into her arms. Her eyes streamed, but she did not say a word. The water in the barrel was still, and the animal's soul was silent.

Dad looked at the screen porch where we watched, wearing a callous grin. Pulling the wet bag from the barrel, he stepped back to avoid further soaking his boots. The sound of mowers and squirrels chirping over a stolen acorn filled the void. Dad held the bag at arm's length, still grinning as he carried the body from our view.

My mother did not find a single scream or reprimand to speak over the scene. She saved her voice for the boy in the den. The cat's fate was sad. But it was not the source of her tears. It was the future of her children that washed her cheeks and stole her voice.

I tore out of my mother's arms to the front window in my room. The useless hag called hope ran with me. Dad opened the bag, dumping its limp contents into the same trash can he had hauled to the curb that morning.

Glimpsing a tiny tuft of butterscotch and white fur as he dropped the dead animal, I watched him slam the lid, triumphant. Listening to the ticking of my windup, smiley alarm clock, I stared at the can, hoping for movement. I prayed for the same sort of resurrection I'd learned about in Sunday school. When my knees, scratched from the porch cement, joined the needles stabbing my stomach, I abandoned the vigil. Splayed out on the ruffled, white comforter of my twin bed, I wore myself out sobbing.

I heard the extended swoosh of the sliding glass door and Dad stepping into the den where Peter sat, still in his pajamas, staring at the television. I hurried to my feet, flying down the hall in time to stand between Dad's temper and my brother. Mom entered from the porch, her eyes rimmed red.

Dad looked at my drawn shoulders and devastation as if I were an annoying crumb he might wipe from his shirt. The puffiness of my cheeks belied the defiance of my carriage. He turned to Peter, the merriment of his accomplishment fading with the whistle of the TV.

"Turn that down, you idiot. What are you people, fuckin' deaf?"

Peter crawled quickly, turning it off. I stared into the bloodshot whites of Dad's milky eyes and answered. "I wish he WAS deaf, Daddy."

He pursed his bottom lip, annoyed at my insolence. Lifting a disapproving eyebrow, he declared, "I'm taking a shower. My socks are soaked." Bending to release his water-logged feet, he asked, "Does a man get lunch around here?"

Mom was pulling cold cuts from the fridge before Dad had removed the second boot.

Later that day, when Dad drove to the hardware store for barbed wire to dissuade other animals from entering his woods, I crept to the trash can. Placing my hand on the sun-warmed metal cover, I considered checking the corpse to be sure it was dead, and I decided against it. It was easy to picture myself or my father dead, but the cat was too much. I imagined its eyes popped like a cartoon clock, claws extended in fright. Rather than look at the dead cat, I recited the Lord's Prayer over the closed lid.

Former beauty queen Donna Deetham's convertible approached. I bent, pretending to tie my shoe. I completed the prayer as soon as the crimson taillights disappeared around the bend. "Dear Lord, please watch over the cat my father killed and kill him as quickly as possible."

17 The Killing Closet

Leaning on the windowsill, I watched for the garbage truck. Sick anticipation and morbid curiosity accompanied me. Would the men see the carcass and report us for animal cruelty? Would the cat look bloated and gory as the workers dumped it into its trashy grave?

When the squeal of truck brakes sounded, I quickly pulled my arms from the painted surface, painfully snagging the stuck skin that my sweat had adhered to the sill. When the truck arrived, the man hanging from the back stopped to wipe his forehead with his uniform sleeve before reaching the lid of the silver can.

I gasped when he dropped it on the lawn, swinging the can in such a fluid movement that its contents looked like a mosaic wave falling into a rainbow. The cat was in the tumbling spectrum, but I could not distinguish its shape among the empty egg cartons, aluminum cans, and cereal boxes. The garbage man turned to drop the can back on our lawn without bothering to cover it. He grabbed the bar, stepping back up to ride on the truck.

I held my breath, hoping the dead animal had landed atop the pile of life's leftovers. His gloved hand slapped the side of the vehicle twice, indicating that the driver should move forward. He did not see it. The cat died, becoming a secret, invisible corpse to everyone except me.

Fury bubbled up, as it did in the moments when I thought too hard about my father. I tried not to think of him without thinking of my mother and brother. As long as they were in my thoughts, running away to find my real family was not an option. I had a job to do, and protecting them was my sanity.

My cheeks grew hot as I slinked to the carpet. My heart galloped with sad thoughts of my entrapment in someone else's life. Why them? Why couldn't we be adopted into another family? *I have to end it*, I thought. *Mom's never going to leave.*

As the cat's carcass churned unnoticed in the refuse-filled truck, the plan I'd playacted for a year crystallized as my one option. Dad was coming home in an hour, and I would be waiting.

At precisely 5:20, I slid into the hall closet, a narrow space where we stored our winter coats, umbrellas, boots, and the shotgun Daddy had used to shoot at the neighbor's Great Dane the year before. Despite Dad's determined aim, brought on by an unacceptable bout of barking, all three shots missed the gentle giant we once rode like a pony. I inspected how Dad cleaned the gun that night, cocking, loading, and uncocking. So, I was sure that I could load the weapon if the time came that I needed to. Killing him was the only option I had not tried.

From my hiding place, I heard the pendulum click on the German cuckoo clock that hung on the dining room wall adjacent to the closet. I listened, hoping that the rhythm would steady the quiver of my hands before I reached for the smooth leather case. Running my finger along the zipper, I grasped the pull, hauling the shotgun to my lap as I freed it from the case.

Polished to a gleam, the grain of the weapon would have seemed pretty if it were not my father's. The gun's weight on my lap felt heavier than all the times that I'd chickened out, replaced the weapon, and slipped out of the closet unnoticed.

No wimping out again, I thought, rocking along with the pendulum as it continued its timekeeping duty. *No tears,* I warned myself, picturing the cat's dead eyes. *Stay angry. Stay strong.*

The air in the closet grew warm, and the chemical smell of the black rubber shoe covers at my side choked me. Pulling them from under my butt, I laid them in a neat pile at the far corner of the space. I removed the ammunition box from the gun case, jiggling it to ensure it was not empty. Three casings rattled against each other, and I opened the box to choose the one I would use. Eenie, Meenie, Miney, Mo, I lifted the cartridge to smell it. I'd done the same the day Dad shot at the Great Dane, finding the discarded casing under the cypress tree Dad had planted for privacy when we moved to Medford. The fresh casing had a different aroma, like a metal watering can full of hose water. The Great Dane casing had smelled like a burnt Fourth of July sparkler.

Uncocking the gun, I placed the red cartridge in the chamber, carefully sliding it shut before closing it. The weapon was ready.

Dad's woolen dress coat scratched my cheek as I turned the gun on its end. Making room, I opened the accordion hinge a sliver and lowered the gun, poking the barrel out the opening. I could not get him from there, and I would have to slide out and peek around the corner towards the front door for proper aim.

As I slid out on my knees, the cuckoo sounded a single musical chime that made me jump. It was 5:30, and Dad would pull into the drive any minute. Mom and Peter were downstairs working on a baseball jigsaw puzzle between washing and folding Dad's work clothes. *Plenty of time,* I thought, as I pulled myself across the oak flooring. *When they come up, he'll be gone.*

The sound of his truck pulling into the drive sent another wave of heat through me; my hands felt slippery on the gun. I tugged at my Bee Gees shirt, dried my palms, and replaced my finger on the trigger. As

I waited to pull back my finger and end my father's life, I wondered what it would be like to exist without constantly wondering who he would kill first.

I twisted my waist around the corner, facing the front screen door. Low sun in the late-day sky cast a shadow across the stoop. *What's taking him so long?* I looked up at the framed photo collage full of the fake smirks we wore to seem like a healthy family. "Liars," I whispered, my heart flip-flopping and my hands growing moister by the second.

I studied the crucifix as I waited. A present from Mom's father, the mother-of-pearl inlay and intricate gold scrollwork shone luminescent behind Jesus's outstretched arms and nailed feet. Above him was a small plaque with the word INRI, and threaded behind his head rested a long-dried palm leaf from a long ago Sunday before church attendance was forbidden.

Gripping the gun, I examined the closed eyes and emaciation of the holy figure. I wondered if God had heard any of my prayers. *My voice probably sounds tiny in this big world*, I thought.

As soon as the observation rose in my head, I saw the movement. So evanescent that it felt imagined, I shivered as if porcelain Jesus had spoken. The awe that filled me was more significant than the one I'd experienced watching faithful parishioners light prayer votives at the back of St. Patrick's Cathedral in the city. My heart revved, and my head grew heavy with the weight of the emotion. Relieved of the deadly duty, I fell to my knees, the trance broken.

I shook my head. I was getting carried away. Jesus could not move any more than he could reach out his arms and steady the trembling that overtook me. Three panicked breaths and the garage door closing filled my ears. I lowered the gun, extremely aware of my vulnerable location. After a glance back at the crucifix, I retreated in a flash, sure my father would notice as he opened the front screen door. The heavy pounding of his work boots vibrated the closet door as he entered the hall. I managed to slide the door shut as he turned the corner. Frozen, with tears welling in my eyes, I held my breath, praying he would not find me. *God heard me*, I thought, as my adrenaline surged. All at once, I smelled mothballs tucked in a shoebox of winter mittens, felt the boot heel wedged against the arch of my bare foot, and heard the hum of the brown fridge as it worked at cooling the banana pudding Mom whipped up for an afternoon snack.

Dad passed my hiding place, heading towards the den. "Where the fuck is everyone?" he yelled.

Clasping the gun to my chest, I waited for the reassuring sound of my mother's voice. Instead, the noise of clattering dishes rattled me further.

"What the fuck does she do all day?" Dad roared.

"Well, I'm taking a shower if anyone gives a rat's ass," he said, pausing outside the coat closet where I thought I would faint from fear. Dad moved on.

I waited until I heard the bathroom door close before tackling the essential task of removing the cartridge from the gun to put it back in the box with its killing cohorts. Carefully inserting the gun in the case and rezipping it gradually to avoid making noise, I propped the weapon butt-down at the exact angle I'd found it.

I swallowed hard, my mouth a desert and my throat thick with anxiety. Peter's laughter made me jump as he ran up the basement stairs and back down. *Mom called him back to clean up*, I thought as I exited the closet. My head reeled, nausea bubbling as I tiptoed to my room, shut the door, and grimaced at the inevitable click of the latch.

Placing the needle of my record player on the black vinyl, I fell to the bedspread and sobbed. "Staying alive, ah, ah, ah," The Bee Gees crooned from my favorite album as I wept for the beatings that would come because I had failed and with relief that I would not go to jail.

Hurt your father, hurt yourself was all I could think as I lay there with my mouth deep in the lace sham to mask the sound. *Did I imagine the movement? Am I going crazy? If I don't stop Dad, who will?* Unanswerable questions flooded my head until I heard my father yell from the hall, "Turn that shit down."

I sat up, dragged the needle across the album, which made the audible scratch he hated, and dried my eyes.

18 Ice

A child's frost-numbed limbs regain sensitivity when stroked by compassion. Venturing from the Medford house after I failed to kill my father was like running away in a slow-motion tiptoe. Every leaving—especially sans parents—had the possibility of being forever.

Rare is a snowstorm in my chosen home of Savannah, but never can I witness the breathtaking beauty of fresh frozen white without recalling the woman who once took my brother and me in from the cold. Her reaction when I told her Dad did not love us seemed strange at first since his parenting was the only thing I knew.

When I let our secret slip, the stranger's shocked expression was a barometer on which I reset parental expectations. He should have been kind. He should have given hugs. He should have lifted Peter and me up, protecting us from every squall. Instead, Dad was the storm.

I now understand his inability to express love for the hiding that it was. I am less demanding of his memory. I still mourn the missing parts of my childhood, the moments that should have embraced my spirit rather than squashing it. I now reflect on strangers like our snowstorm lady as angels lighting the way so we could know something better existed.

I wish I could hug her, the seraph who saved us for that beautiful hour all those years ago. Perhaps, she will read this and know that a moment of kindness can last a lifetime.

~ ~ ~

Crisp auburn leaves dangled from the maple tree in our yard, as surprised as the residents of Medford at the blanket of snow that covered the quiet streets. The cold snap surprise turned my mind to skating. With sparkly ice skates still untouched in their boxes from the Christmas before, I was determined to try them out. I was finally old enough to walk to the pond, a man-made flooded area at the middle school. The temperature that November Sunday shivered at an icy twenty-eight degrees.

"Come on, Mom; we haven't used our skates once. We'll grow out of them if we don't use them soon." I begged Mom to let us venture into the pristine white of the early afternoon snowfall.

"It's freezing. I'm not sure." Mom rested her wrist on her hip, as was her habit right before saying yes. The noon whistle used to notify volunteer firefighters of a fire on the Island sounded, its steady bellow so familiar that we hardly noticed.

"We'll wear our ski pants, and I promise Peter will keep his hood on."

"Alright, but be back by two o'clock; you hear me?" I burst down the hall, stopping to shout into Peter's room, "Get your snowsuit, Peter, we're going skating!"

"Okay, can you help me?" Peter stopped playing, sliding his wind-up train under the bed to avoid the beating that accompanied anything untidy.

"Yep." I pulled Peter's snowsuit from the bottom drawer of his dresser. Mom entered carrying a couple of clear vegetable baggies. "You'll need these over your socks to keep your feet dry. Go get ready," she told me, "I'll help your brother."

108

I raced to grab my snow pants and boots, sitting on my bed to get them over my denim pants. By the time I finished layering, I could not bend to pull on my black boots. I wobbled stiffly at the center of my room, laughing at my robot-like movements.

"Mom, can you get my boots on? I can't bend."

"Of course, honey." Mom had me lean against the bathroom counter while she pulled the boots over thick socks and baggies.

Mom took a photo of us on the front stoop before we headed off on our icy adventure. I carried both sets of double-blade skates over my shoulder, holding Peter's mitten-covered hand most of the way to the pond. An eerie quiet accompanied us. "Looks like it's snowing again." Delighted, Peter tugged on my hand, urging me to move faster.

We walked to the edge of the neighborhood, extending our tongues and giggling. It was a competition to see who would catch the biggest flake of fluffy coldness. At Sunburst Drive, we passed through a well-traversed shortcut through the yard of a long-abandoned dump we called Miller's place. Whether a Miller family ever lived there mattered little to the neighborhood kids who double dared each other to enter the half-furnished dwelling. As we passed the busier road, I grew more aware, pulling Peter close and keeping him from the street traffic.

Away from the homes of neighbors whose names we knew, our steps quickened. We arrived at the hilly mounds of the park, and the pond came into view. Peter let loose, dropping onto the virgin snow to wave his arms and legs, making a snow angel.

I bent to help him put on his skates, then donned my own. Leaving the four baggies from our boots on a bench near the pond, we held hands for balance as we approached the frozen surface. We were alone. Most families were at church at 12:30 on Sunday. We had attended Sunday school for several years but stopped after Dad tore up Mom's collection envelopes on her nightstand. Dad demanded they stop spending money on "all that church bullshit." Mom decided it would be immoral and embarrassing to attend without adding something to the collection plate.

Venturing out on the shallow ice, we giggled at the wobble of our legs. Peter fell forward on his well-cushioned knees, gathering snow to toss at me. Staggering my way to one knee, I returned the favor. We skated, tumbled, and giggled—the echo of our joy interrupting the muffled stillness of nature's tranquil freeze.

At the bank, we gathered snow into high piles of fluff. Uncooperative, the snow flew around us, cascading from our pile. We managed to amass a slouching anthill of white, sticking broken branches into its sides for arms. Peter fell back, laughing at the pathetic appearance of our snowman. I noticed the over-pink hue of Peter's cheeks and checked my Cinderella watch for the time. It was 1:40.

"We better get going. Mom said to be home by two. I'm getting cold."

Peter nodded, pulling his blue knit scarf higher over his cheeks. "Me too."

Stepping back across the ice, we slid to the bench where we'd left our boots. "Uh-oh." Peter worried when he spotted the blanket of snow that covered them.

"Oh no." I lifted the boots in a panic, shaking snow from the plastic bags and linings of our boots. "We can't walk home in these," I pointed to my skates. "We gotta put the boots on. It's gonna be cold, but we're not that far." I tried to assure Peter.

"I don't want to wear them." He resisted my effort to unlace his skates.

"You have to," I admonished. "Stop wiggling."

"Nooo." Peter kicked again before giving in.

Spilling snow from the baggies and deciding them useless, I shoved them into the zipper pockets of my coat and slid Peter's boots over his wet socks. "It hurts," Peter complained.

As whenever he showed any sign of pain, I touched my face. *It's too cold to melt*, I assured myself. Pulling on my boots as fast as I could, I tied the laces of our skates to throw over my shoulder. The snow fell more quickly, sticking to our eyelashes and making it hard to see.

A few yards from the pond, Peter started to cry. "My feet hurt. I can't walk. It burns."

I felt the same sting as the moisture inside my boots turned to ice. The temperature was dropping, and we were still many blocks from home. "Carry me?" Peter asked, but I could only manage a few feet with Peter in my arms. When I sat him down, he cried harder, miserable at the pain in his feet.

I stood, the weight of our predicament churning in my stomach. Accustomed to guarding Peter against my father's fists but unprepared for nature's fury, I had no idea what to do. The enemy was all around us, the cold too much for his little feet and nary another soul in sight.

Peter sat down for the third time, refusing to budge. The idea of knocking at the door of one of the white-sided homes we passed frightened me practically as much as the prospect of frostbite.

I chose the house due to its lit porch light. Hiding my unsteadiness from Peter, I pulled off my mitten to press the doorbell. The sound lit in a sing-song chime. I nudged Peter behind me, just in case.

A woman opened the front door a sliver. "Yes?" she asked, her eyes appeared cautious.

"We were skating. We got snow in our boots. My brother can't walk. I need to get him home." I spat out the words, weighed down by my inability to protect him. Embarrassed, I shivered, fearing we already had frostbite. My toes hurt so bad I wanted to cry.

111

"Oh my, of course. Come in, get those boots off, and we'll call your parents." The gray-haired woman pointed to a mat near the door. I peeled off Peter's snow boots and sopping wet socks, opening his coat, too, as the room was too warm for our snow garments. Peter sat rubbing his toes while I removed my boots and socks. Judging by the pain, I expected my toes would be black. Instead, the screaming skin wore the assaulting tone of an over-ripe watermelon.

"That's better," the woman said, watching from the distance of a stranger. "Come into the kitchen and call your mother, and I'll make cocoa."

I lifted the yellow phone from the wall to dial, watching impatiently as the rotary dial spun back from the final seven. "Hello."

It was Dad. My heart sank. I almost hung up, not wanting to get in trouble for being with a stranger. Gathering my nerve, I answered, "Hi, Dad, is Mom there?"

"Where are you? You're supposed to be skating."

"We were, but Peter's boots filled with snow, and he couldn't walk, so we stopped."

Dad slowed his speech, enunciating each word severely. "I asked you a question. Where... are... you...?"

"Um, we stopped at a lady's house, and she said we could call Mom." I watched the stranger pour steaming water into two cups, spooning in heaping spoons full of powder from the familiar yellow box with the chocolate bunny smiling back.

"She's making us hot chocolate," I added, smiling in anticipation of the warm goodness.

"Give her the phone now," Dad barked.

I covered the mouthpiece with her hand, "It's my Dad. He's mad. Wants to talk to you."

The woman set the mugs in front of us, nodding to indicate that we should sit and drink.

I unzipped my coat, and lifting the cup to my cold lips, swallowed, savoring the heated relief that traveled down my throat. I looked at Peter, who was slurping as he sipped. He wore a brown cocoa mustache that made me laugh.

The woman gave Dad her address, assuring him that we were okay. I could tell Dad had hung up before she could say goodbye because she stared at the phone in her hand.

Noticing we were watching, she smiled gently, asking, "Want some more? Your father will be here soon."

"Thanks for letting us in. We had better get our boots back on. Dad doesn't like to wait."

Peter stopped mid-slurp. "I'm not putting them back on."

"You have to, Peter. Dad's coming." He frowned.

"I'm sure your Dad could carry him; maybe I could get you some of my husband's socks. You can return them anytime."

"Dad won't carry him. He hates us," the words slipped. The woman's friendly expression turned to horror, and I realized that while it was the truth, it was not a truth I should share with strangers.

"Surely, he. I mean." The woman looked back at the phone, likely recalling the abrupt hang-up. "Well, let's get some warm socks and tuck some newspaper in those boots. You'll be just fine."

Dad pulled into the drive, laying on the truck horn to tell us he had arrived. We left with borrowed socks, delightfully warmed tummies, and the woman's good wishes. "Thank you so much, I croaked, tearing up as I looked from her gauzy expression of compassion to our father's angry face.

"Why, of course, it wouldn't be right to leave two kids out in this." She waved at the snow, and for a moment, I thought she might erase it with her gentleness.

Dad drove us home in silence. When we got to the house, the driveway was a blanket of fresh white. We got out of the truck as fast as we could, afraid of the punishment we knew Dad would dole out at any moment.

I grabbed our ice skates from the floor. Dad stopped me before I could exit, putting his hand out to take them.

"I'll put them away, Daddy," I said, trying to relieve the tension of the moment.

"No, you won't. I told your mother you were too young for the goddamn skates, and look what happened. Hand 'em over."

"Why, Dad? It started snowing. We had fun. We did. Our feet got wet, and it was too cold." I held the skates close.

"Now," he demanded.

Peter let out a fearful whimper, and I handed them over.

Dad left us to get out of the truck on our own. Pounding down the drive to the trash can, he opened it. Depositing the skates, he slammed it shut.

Peter began to cry. I glared at our father as he passed us. Mom was at the door when we went in, ready to deliver big hugs and warm us up. Dad ignored her pampering, heading to the basement to bang nails into the wall frames he was forever finishing.

I snuggled in the luxury of Mom's embrace but did not cry. After changing into dry clothes, our stomachs full of canned chicken noodle soup, I went to my room.

Behind the closed door, defiance fell away. In its place grew fearful images of what might have been. I shed tears at the loss of my skates and unanswered prayers.

Somehow, even as my father defiled our childhood, I believed my God was transcendent, his majesty not bound by my Daddy's rules. So, I prayed again, "Lord, I'm sorry we got snow in our boots. Please let my father die soon."

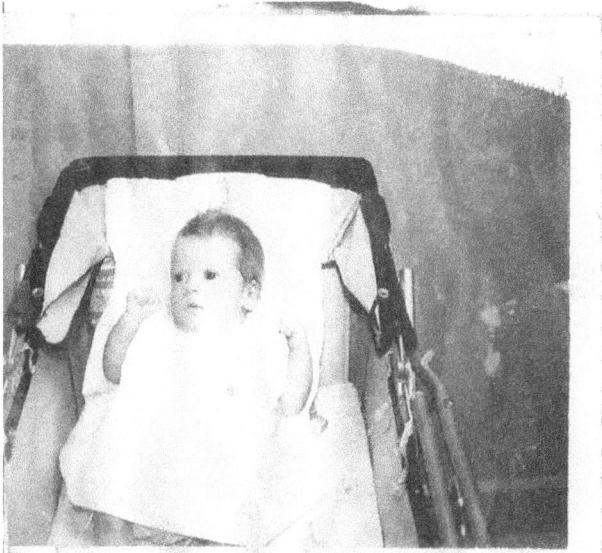

NYC Adoption file photo: the only pre-adoption photo of Vicki-lynn (1965)

Joe and Lillian NYC (1964) Vicki-lynn, age 26 months

Lillian, Joe and Vicki-lynn (early 1960s)

Joe, Lillian, and Vicki-lynn (early 1960s)

Vicki-lynn and Peter

Vicki-lynn & Peter: Christmas morning (early 1970s)

The Selbach family (1970s)

Image Joann mailed to Vicki-lynn after gender affirmation surgery

19 Gnashing

Sometimes a fleeting moment holds the truth you've missed for a lifetime.

In late October 1976, Dad emerged from my parent's room wearing Mom's loosest dress, a string of pearls too tight at his neck, and clip-on earrings that pulled his earlobes low. Carrying the same old-fashioned purse Mom had borrowed from her mother when they first met, he smiled an uncharacteristically wide grin. Peter and I giggled at the get-up he would wear to a friend's Halloween party. Had we been allowed to attend the adult-only party, I wonder if we would have spotted the authenticity of our father's outfit. I never saw Dad dress up for Halloween before that night, nor after. It was a singular event with stunning consequences.

Did that momentary emergence of Dad's hidden gender spur the vicious cycle of the next few months? I think so. Perhaps, Dad's truth became clearer after he wore it among friends. To experience freedom and acceptance for something you have hidden for so long must have felt jubilant. To redon the armor of manhood must have weighed on him, making the secret an even heavier burden.

There is no excuse for abuse, and I am not defending it. I am simply considering the spark that likely ignited our harshest winter.

One month after our ice skates suffered the same fate as the Calico, the bloodletting escalated.

Mom left ash from her morning smoke in the amber glass ashtray.

"You want to die, don't you?" Dad asked, grabbing her hair with one hand and lifting the ashtray to her nose with the other. It was a question that, in any different situation, would deserve serious consideration. But for us, the frequency of the inquiry morphed the promise of death into a prediction of blood.

"No, Joe. Please," she lifted her arms to cover her face, and Dad repeatedly slammed the ashtray into her neck and shoulder until she fell to the floor. He kicked her next.

I saw the football size bruises the next day at Sears when Mom brought Peter and me into the dressing room. "Turn around," she ordered as she tried on a blue turtleneck top she hoped would cover the evidence. I peeked at the reflection in the mirror, sickened by the purple wounds on her neck, chest, and side.

~ ~ ~

Peter left a purple plastic racing car on the floor beside his bed.

He rushed to put it away, crossing as far from Daddy as possible. Dad caught him, throwing his frightened frame to the bed. "You like this, making me hit you? You're an idiot. Probably had idiot parents. You little pansy."

Peter pulled down his pants without being told. Dad smiled as he whipped the belt across his nude behind, leaving lashes so severe that my brother would have to lay on his side for two days.

~ ~ ~

120

Mom moved Dad's wallet from its usual spot on the dresser.

"Trying to steal my money? You whore." He closed the bedroom and bathroom doors. I slept as he repeatedly slammed her head into the shower door until her forehead split, and she passed out.

I found Mom on the blue bathmat the following day, "I was sick last night," she lied. "Must have been the pork roast. Fell asleep."

I might have believed her if not for the fissure on her forehead and the African-shaped brown blood stain on the mat where her head bled. I looked at the tub, wishing I could fill it and immerse myself in its warmth. I found peace underwater, the one place where I could not hear the things that made me most afraid.

It was the year of a thousand bruises. I hoped it would end on my birthday, which had always been an unspoken truce. Dad loved me on my birthday. But, in the year of our ultimate evil, he forgot.

That Christmas Eve, a full moon lit my room, making the long wait for sleep more bearable. I was afraid of the dark. More precisely, I feared who my father might hurt while I slept under the black cover of night.

I went to bed ahead of Peter. Exhausted, I lay in my bed, one hand on my face, sure the heat of my anxiety would cause the skin to fall away, waxen, and dead. I listened to the house settle and the sound of Peter following our bedtime rituals.

Daddy defined our bedtime procedure with precise steps. First, you washed your hands and face. Then, you cleaned the bar of soap and folded the washcloth on the chrome loop. Next, you brushed your teeth, counting to twenty in your head. We were permitted to go to bed once the sink area was spotless and the ritual was complete.

I must have fallen asleep. I awoke to a roar of pain from the bathroom we shared with our parents. Peter had missed a step. The trembling of my limbs amplified as I flew down the hall, arriving to see

121

the first drop of blood hit the tiles. Peter writhed, yowling. Blood dripped from his raw gums like a broken faucet.

Dad towered over my brother's taut agony, scraping his tiny teeth with the blue dinosaur toothbrush Peter had received at his last dental appointment. The pink of his gums disappeared under blood-soaked bristles. "That'll teach you to brush your goddamn teeth, dumb ass."

"Stop, Daddy, please," my hand was on his monstrous arm, tugging down from the elbow. He was too solid, despite my hanging from his arm with all my weight. With a wad of Peter's hair in his hand, he tugged back to better access the teeth he deemed unworthy of sleep.

I struggled with Dad, swiping wildly at his head, too far from my reach. The memory of my birthday candles faded as I swatted again and again.

"Mooooooommmmmmmmmm," I screamed, at once regretting it. I needed an adult's help, but calling Mom to the scene would put her in danger.

Mom was in the basement retrieving her bathrobe from the dryer when she heard me scream. She arrived stunned, "Joe, it's Christmas Eve. What are you doing?" The frivolity and bright colors of our matching striped pajamas and nightgowns, chosen especially for Christmas Eve, contradicted the serious scene.

Dad looked up, releasing Peter's collar. My brother scurried across the floor, diving through Mom's legs to run to his room. I grabbed a washcloth from the towel ring, following him. Peter sucked hungrily on the cloth, gagging several times from the taste of his blood.

I whispered, "It's Christmas tomorrow, Peter. Nothing bad ever happens on Christmas. Santa's coming." I lied, trying to sound convincing despite the blood that oozed through my fingers. In the years before we moved to the three-bedroom house in Medford, my birthday had been a shiny respite from the dark. Like a well-placed speed bump, my Christmas Eve birthday usually decelerated my father's passionate evil. I lay there with Peter wondering why Dad had loved me so freely in the years before causing my mother and brother pain had become the driving force of everything. What had I done to turn this birthday sour?

"Where's Santa?" Peter asked, looking out his window for the fat man he believed would come down the front path since we had no fireplace. Moonlight bathed the room in a false illumination of hope.

I rocked my brother, "Do you think he'll eat the cookies we left? I do. Bet you, he'll be here soon, and Santa might not even fit through the front door with all those presents."

The cloth fell to my lap as Peter's mouth relaxed in sleep. His gums looked swollen, wrecked by the bent bristles and rubbing of the hard plastic. I caught my breath, tucked him in, and closed his door, listening to my parents yelling in the hall.

"He's a little boy, Joe," Mom pleaded from the master bedroom.

"He's a pig. Gets it from you, I see." Dad was still in the bathroom, cleaning blood from the sink and floor. "Look at this crap. The floor is filthy. You come from a sty, fat piggy? You and the kids mess up everything you touch."

"I just mopped it Monday," she answered from bed, her voice weary. I thought about her exhausted tone, deciding it came from wrapping gifts, baking cookies, and the constant struggle of being married to Dad.

"Well, today is Thursday, Lillian. Four fucking days. Get in here, NOW. Or I'm gonna scrub your face with my fist."

I heard Mom's slippers shuffle across the hardwood floor as she approached the doorway.

"Look at this crap," screamed Dad.

Mom did not answer, and something about her silence compelled me to inch toward the bathroom door. It was open when I peeked in.

Dad had the bloody towel pushed to Mom's face, obstructing her nose and mouth. Unable to breathe, I watched her fall to her knees.

Preying on her low position, Dad let go of the towel to grab her curls with both hands. Hurling her towards the toilet, he slammed her face on the porcelain bowl three times before immersing her head in the water. Mom moaned, and I heard her breath bubble at the surface.

Fed up and fuming with adrenaline, I crossed to the corner of Peter's room where his finally useful baseball bat rested. Taking the bat in hand, I closed his door, lifting the weapon over my head. My heart slammed against my ribcage as I entered the bathroom swinging. I had no idea what I might strike as blind rage engulfed me. I had to end him. The weight of the first wide swing knocked the extra roll of toilet paper with the crocheted doll cover from the partition between the sink and toilet.

Dad ducked, releasing Mom, who came up for air, gagging and spitting. My next swing landed on Dad's arm, which he'd raised in defense. "Why are you doing this?" he asked in the victim's voice; he slung on like a holster after every battle. I lost my footing then, which softened the impact on my father's hand to a mere tap. He squealed like a newborn pup, grabbing his barely bruised hand with the other.

Mom sat on the toilet in a trance, staring at the cheap butterfly print on the wall. Dad howled, "Look what you made her do. You turned my daughter against me. You see this, you bitch?"

I grabbed my stomach, the angry scream of the ulcer and seism of my muscles nearly bringing me to my knees. My voice ricocheted through the bathroom. "It's you, Dad. It's always you. You're evil. I hate you. We all hate you." The powerful words poured from me like sweat in a fever.

Dad stopped his venomous blaming to look at me. The mask of hate melted into pitiful mourning of false accusation. He tightened the drawstring waist of his red and green pajamas, which had loosened in

124

the melee. I raised the bat again, sure he would punish my mother for my tirade.

Dad turned away from my accusatory stare, his voice deflated. "All you had to do is clean the fucking bathroom. Now, look what you did. See what you did to my daughter." He pushed past me, leaving through the master bedroom, heading to the sulking throne where he habitually rocked away his perceived wounds after doling out a beating.

"My daughter. Look what you did. You made her hate me," he mumbled over the indignant creak of the rocking chair.

Inside the bathroom, I coaxed my mother to her feet, helping her rinse away the blood. Patting her cheeks dry, I watched her retreat to the semi-conscious state that was her refuge. Her eyes were open, but she did not see me.

Guiding her to her side of the bed, I kissed her forehead before pulling the blanket over her motionless body. She stared at the ceiling, not blinking at my father's rant in the other room.

"You made them hate me, you bitch," Dad chanted a spent soliloquy. "You turned dem against me."

After laying my head on Mom's chest to check for breath, I left my parent's room to check on Peter. Peter stirred as I shut the door, "Santa?" he asked as I caught my breath, wiping away tears to hide my upset.

"Yes, Peter, Santa," I lied, wondering if there would be any gifts under the tree. Spooning my brother's back in the twin bed, we slept five hours as the malevolence of my birthday morphed into Christmas.

I woke with Peter's finger poking the small of my back, "It's light out. Let's go see."

With one more nightmare behind us, I agreed. "Sure, we gotta get Mom and Dad up, though." The rules for Christmas morning were as strict as every other day. We were to wake our parents before approaching the seven-foot artificial tree in the den. We were not to look at or touch a single item, or we would have to watch Dad burn our gifts on the grill.

"Wait here for a sec," I warned Peter. He shrugged his shoulders, peering down the hall anxiously.

I tip-toed into our parent's room, "Can we go see our presents, Mom?" Mom nodded at my whispered request.

"Sure, honey." Mom turned away from me, revealing a garish purple bruise on her shoulder where her nightgown had fallen.

Dad's side of the bed was empty.

The smell of coffee and blueberry blintzes greeted us in the den. My father sat pasting green stamps into the S & H Quick Saver book. The S & H catalog was one of our favorite pastimes. Peter and I put tiny check marks next to our wishes in the book. He wanted the Nylint Model T Car, and I dreamed of the Lapin Strummer Guitar. Dad just laughed whenever we chose prizes. He was saving up for the Precision Lawn Spreader.

I rubbed my eyes as the late night had not afforded me much sleep. Peter tugged at my sleeve, spotting the untried bikes and mass of wrapped presents beside the blue-lit tree. Underneath the tree, our traditional village of cardboard Christmas houses sparkled over the cotton snow and plastic people.

"Santa did it," I looked at Dad, who was licking a stamp to add to the book. I could not believe either of my parents had fashioned such normality. Only a drop of dried blood on Peter's collar and the bubbling singe of my melting face exposed the truth of the night before.

Bulging stockings stuffed with candy canes, yo-yos, and silly putty hung on the cardboard fireplace. Mom arrived wrapped in her purple robe, the white one no longer wearable for the blood stains. She switched on the television, tuning it to the Yuletide channel. A roaring fireplace came into view.

Mom retrieved the Golden brand blueberry blintzes from the stove and sour and whipped creams from the fridge, setting them near Dad, who shoved the stamps back into the envelope he used to save them. As soon as he shelved the stamps and book, we sat to devour the sweet treats that were a Christmas tradition.

"Slow down," I laughed at Peter, who shoved an entire Blintz into his mouth.

"The presents aren't going anywhere," Mom assured, sipping her coffee.

"Done." Peter raised his hands in victory as he finished the last mouthful of blueberry, wiping his hands and staring me into a quick last bite of my breakfast.

"Wash your hands, then go," Dad said, busy setting his watch. He tapped at the glass dial. "This ding ain't half bad. Guess your Mom likes me all right now. Nice gift."

The fake glow of the television fireplace burned in the background as we unwrapped present after present. Dad snapped photos on slide film as we tossed wrapping paper. Mom applauded for every gift. Twister, Monopoly, Don't Break the Ice; the games kept coming as the flash bulb rotated atop Dad's camera.

"I got a Tonka, Vicki," Peter crooned, sliding his hand under the truck's carriage to roll it towards me.

"You have one more to open." I pointed, slinking to the carpet, exhausted.

As soon as the last gift was opened, Dad gathered the heaping pile of wrapping paper in a plastic trash bag. Peter revved up a plastic car, crawling to lead it around the Christmas village. Mom stretched across the couch.

Christmas morning faded into a day of play and napping.

20 Brains

If you look up long enough, you're bound to spot an angel.

~ ~ ~

When your father drowns cats, and your home is habitually dissonant, fairy tales become eerily plausible. That spring, as daffodils popped from the still-cold earth, my sweet tooth became the victim of a delicious tug on a Sugar Daddy candy.

I was a tad ancient for all that tooth fairy silliness. But I slid the tooth under my pink pillow anyway, hopeful for a fifty-cent piece to add to the copper pig I was filling for when I'd run away with my brother.

An hour or so after I fell asleep, something stirred me. I pried my eyes open, wiping the sleep from them. Thinking I might still be asleep, I spotted the impossible interloper near the window. She appeared in full regalia of blue with flowing blonde locks. Instinctively, I stuck my tongue in the empty tooth socket, tasting the rusty blood of the loss. Sliding my hand under my pillow to look for it, I pulled a coin from the warm sheet, the flowy vision disintegrating when I looked back at the window.

My room was dark. *Must have been a dream?* I thought as I settled back under the covers. Just then, a ball of blue phosphorescence bounced outside my bedroom window.

Wake up, ding-dong, I thought, rising to part the priscilla curtains to look for signs of the much more likely police car, or whatever was causing the bouncing glow. Through the window, I found the source of the light. It was coming from the Kim's house next door.

Our neighbors, a Chinese American family, had a meticulously landscaped yard and a neighborhood reputation for being spies. Well, that's what freckle-faced boss-boy Greg Deetham told us kids, and since Greg was rarely mistaken, we believed him.

Greg lived one block away on Richmond Avenue with his sister Patty and his parents, Greg and Donna. I played with his sister Patty often. Everyone wanted to visit the Deethams, mostly because of their sexy, Nancy Sinatra-booted mother.

As hip as they came, Mrs. Deetham wore her hair in a long bob with the ends curled up, and shorty-short sheath dresses that drew men outside to mow the lawn whenever she sunned herself in the front yard. Her husband, Greg Senior, was the same cop who'd welcomed us to the neighborhood during our picnic on the concrete foundation of the house years before.

Dad favored stereotypes. He nicknamed our neighbors "the communists" because they did not speak English, at least not when we were in earshot. The Kims were also night owls. We rarely ever saw them outside before dusk.

Busy with the drama of my own family, I rarely contemplated the Kims' habits. But that night, as the mysterious light moved about their backyard, the idea of them being spies seemed likely. I stared at the light for ten minutes, sliding open the casement window to listen. The faint sound of strange voices and the unmistakable clang of a shovel hitting dirt met my eager ears.

129

"Dear Lord, let them sleep like they're dead," I prayed as I tiptoed past my parent's bedroom, peeking in at Peter who was sound asleep.

Easing the front door open, I winced at the creak of the top hinge, stopping to see if anyone would wake up. No one stirred. So, I eased the screen door open, closing it quietly behind me. The latch of the screen sounded like a sonic boom, freezing me to the concrete stoop.

The cold night air sent a shiver of goosebumps up my arms as I waited for signs of life in my house. Pretty sure it was safe, I shuffled past the rose bushes, careful not to catch my nightgown on the thorny bushes Dad had planted to keep animals and humans away from his garage.

Walking outside my father's house at night made me want to run away. But leaving my brother and mother with him was an unthinkable option. I crept instead, sure that if caught, my father would think I was trying to run away. Where would he hide my remains? I wondered as I peeked through the thin patch of pine and oak trees that separated our yard from the neighbor's. The Kims' moonlit backyard was still now. The bobbing light that had drawn me out of the house was gone.

Inhaling the sweet aroma of Dad's roses, I stared into the Kims' yard, my overactive imagination wondering if a thief might have gagged the neighbors and tied them up inside. I squinted at the yard, slowly inspecting the neat landscape and flower beds for signs of trespass.

Close to their back patio, I spotted a series of circles carved out of the turf. Approaching the chain link, I ducked near a bush to get a closer look. The spots were fresh and about the size of basketballs. There were four.

Satisfied that the Kim family was up to something, I went back to the house, panicking when pulling at the front screen; it stuck for a moment. Wiping my dirty feet on the inside mat, I snuck down the hall to get back in bed.

The next day was Saturday. I weeded the cobblestones at breakneck speed, finishing the path in just over an hour.

"Can I go to Laura's?" I asked Dad.

"Yeah," Dad answered. "I got more chores for you later. Be back at noon."

I sped off on my Huffy, beyond excited to tell Laura, Susan, Kenny, and anyone else who would listen about the midnight activities I'd witnessed.

"So, they woke me up with this weird light, and I found four holes in the ground near their back patio. They are huge, big enough to bury a cat or something." I left out the tooth fairy apparition, not wanting to mess with my credibility.

By four o'clock that afternoon, at least two members of our Huffy gang had biked past the Kims' house looking for clues. We had a mystery to solve, and my friends were happy to help.

While Dad worked in the yard, I drew a map of the place where I saw the holes.

"What's that?" Peter asked, sipping a Yoo-hoo drink.

"Something for school," I said, not wanting to scare him.

"Can I go back to Laura's?" I asked Mom, who was wiping down the counter.

"Sure, clean up your schoolwork first," she answered without turning around.

I flew down the street on my bike, a symphony of lawnmowers escorting me back to Laura's driveway. Laura, her brother, and a few kids who were visiting their grandma listened as I explained the location of the large holes and the light that led me to them.

One of the visiting kids suggested we use tight ropes to gain access to the hole farthest from their back door by dangling and digging with robots. Laura's brother, who was three years older than us, looked mildly amused and volunteered his erector set for the mission; then he burst out laughing.

The schemes and plans of discovering the Kims' clandestine plantings petered as suppertime bells rang. It was a delicious day, for I held a secret that momentarily usurped the Selbachs' reign as the most notorious family in the neighborhood.

Life went on in typical fifth-grade fashion until two Tuesdays later when biking home from Laura's. I spotted Dad standing in the Kims' front yard, holding a large jar and nodding at Mrs. Kim.

Before they could see me, I spun around to head back to Mrs. Anderson's driveway. I must have looked scared as I caught my breath because Laura asked, "Are you okay?"

When your father shoots animals without so much as a muscle twitch, it is easy to believe the worst. "He's holding a head in a jar and talking to Mrs. Kim in broad daylight on her front steps."

We all froze. It was clear from the moment the words fell from my lips that fear is stronger than curiosity. My friends looked at their feet, silenced by the proclamation.

The group scattered, someone suggesting, "You can tell us what happens tomorrow."

I understood my friend's fear. No one wanted to mess with Dad ever since he'd carried his shotgun up and down the block six months prior. Aggravated by the barking of a neighbor's Great Dane, he'd strode up and down the pavement chanting, "Who's gonna stop me? Heh? Who's gonna stop me?" I don't know why the barking set him off that day, but it took two neighbors to convince him to put away the gun and go home.

I rode back to my house, past the Kims' now deserted yard. Dad was gone.

Putting my bike in the garage, I went inside. Pork chops sizzled in the oven.

"Set the table," Mom said.

Peter and I moved into plate-slamming, silverware-placing duty. That's when I spotted the jar. Bigger than the biggest pickle jar I'd ever seen. Taller than the glass milk bottles left in the silver cooler box on our front step and wider than a bathroom wastebasket, the jar sat on the counter next to the fridge, covered with a hand towel. The inside of the jar, at least the part I could see from where I sat, was gooey green and red.

Guts, I thought. Having touched damaged flesh, bandaged seeping wounds, and witnessed my mother and brother being stitched back together, I naturally assumed the worst.

I prayed, "Please don't let him show us," wondering if my father intended to share the gooey contents of the jar as a scare tactic. It would have worked. In fact, I would have weeded every cobblestone from New York to California to avoid touching the gelatinous goo. The contents of the jar looked like decomposed flesh.

Throughout dinner, I eyed the exposed atrocity, hoping it would disappear. After dinner, Dad sat back, looking satisfied, and said, "Oh yeah, there's something I want you to try."

He stood, heading to the jar. I gasped, terrified that he would remove the cover. I shielded Peter's eyes. Dad pulled the towel from atop the pot. It was much worse than I had imagined. It was a green and red mush of flesh. I could not look away, my eyes looking for something recognizable, human. Then it dawned on me. Dad had said, "Try something."

What? He's going to make us eat brains.

Peter pushed my hands away. The cat's howl filled my head, and I believed we were about to become forced cannibals.

When Dad opened the lid, the aroma was as pungent as I expected death would smell after being buried in the dirt for weeks. I almost passed out when Dad grabbed a spoon from the silverware drawer, shoving it into the gelatinous goo. He spooned a big helping into his mouth and began sweating profusely. His face crimson, he waved the spoon in the air and said, "That's pungent shit. Got two jars from Chung. Try some."

Dad put a spoonful near my lips, and the stinging began immediately. *I am dying,* I thought, holding my hand over my mouth to protect it from the offering. "No, Dad, No," I grumbled through my hand.

"Typical; you kids won't try anything different."

Dad continued to scold us for our childish palates, "Try something special, for crap's sake."

Mom cleared the dishes saying, "Too rich for me. I can't stomach it."

No kidding, Mom, it's frigging brains, I thought, standing to help her clean up and hurrying Peter to the den to watch *Gilligan's Island.*

"What the fuck am I going to do with this much Kimchi?" Dad dished up more of the concoction before closing the lid.

Kimchi. Is that who they killed? I wondered.

"I'll rebury it out back to keep it fresh," Dad said, heading out the back door, the huge jar tucked under his arm.

Mom dried dishes chattering as if Dad was still in the room. "I never could take that spicy food. How do those people eat it?"

"What stuff?" I asked Mom.

"Kimchi, didn't you smell it? They make it out of cabbage and spices. Chung Miller buries it in the ground to make the flavor stronger. So hot, it burns your lips before it even touches them. Jean won't eat it, so she gave Dad two jars. He brought one over to the Kims."

Kimchi was not a person. It was food.

Despite relief that my father had not conspired to kill and eat human brains, I ran to the bathroom, where I bent over the commode and vomited.

Still believing that my Dad could kill and eat human brains, I peered through the fence later that day. There, in a pretty row, were four new shrubs along the Kims' back walkway—a green guarantee that quelled my queasy stomach.

21 Keeping Company

Compressed, bluish indentations in the soft flesh of upper arms. Bite marks on breasts and shoulders. Bruised thighs covered by pants purchased with the abuser's money. Hiding was a way of life for suburban housewives in the 1970s. No shelters, help posters, or domestic abuse campaigns existed on Long Island.

Even ugly bruises under puffy eyes were ignored. Look away. Look away, and it's not real. Share whispered truths with the others. The ones who have also learned the art of makeup tricks and clothing camouflage. Battles raged in bedrooms, on kitchen floors, and in mental cages, and we, the children, watched with stitched lips and useless limbs, believing that no amount of telling could free us.

~ ~ ~

April bloomed moderately. An unseasonable warmth awakened tiny buds on rose bushes at the south side of our house. Among the cobblestones, dormant weeds waited to sprout. So, I spent Saturday morning flopped in front of the television, coloring side-by-side pages in the cowboy coloring book Peter had received for his eighth birthday.

I traced the lines of the Indian chief on my page, filling in with a fluorescent green crayon from the seventy-two-count box sandwiched between us. Peter colored over the lines, more interested in the beep of the cartoon bird than coloring.

Dad entered, holding barbecue tongs. Mom looked up from *Reader's Digest.* "Pork Roast tonight. We'll eat outside," Dad announced, opening the door to the back patio. The first warm breeze in months shuffled pages in our coloring book.

"Did you take it out to thaw?" Mom asked.

"Yeah, last night. I heard it was gonna be a warm one. Wanna invite the Deethams?"

I perked up at the suggestion. Having company usually meant a fight-free night.

"Sure. I'll give 'em a call." Mom went to the hall phone to dial. She knew the number by heart since Peter and I were friends with the Deetham's kids.

Mom hung up, returning to tell Dad they would indeed have company. "Donna says they'd love to. The kids are with her parents, so it'll just be her and Greg."

"Great, I better clean da grill. Gotta get the meat on early." The prospect of pork and escaping winter hibernation had put Dad in a chipper mood. Mom went to count the potatoes in the veggie bin. Peter gave up on coloring, and I took the book in my lap to finish my page. I looked at Dad on the porch. With metal brush in hand, he looked up, catching my gaze.

For a moment, he was a typical Dad preparing for a festive dinner with friends. My heart lifted. It was the same helpful, happy look worn by my friend Sofia's dad. The early afternoon sun vivified the den, and I moved to sit in the patch of light, cherishing the moment.

"You kids better get dressed. You still have to fold the towels and clean your rooms." Mom piped in from the kitchen, where she was now peeling the potatoes. Cutting each one and dropping it in a cold bath, she prepped the spuds for boiling and mashing.

Peter turned off the television, sliding down the hall in slippery-footed pajamas. I followed.

When the doorbell rang two hours later, the aroma of roast pork mingled with a starchy buttered goodness that ignited everyone's hunger. Peter and I set the redwood picnic table with Mom's favorite melamine dishes and sharp knives. Dad wanted to eat outside so they could enjoy the warm afternoon.

Dad put down the tongs to answer the door. Greg wore toothy confidence, slim-cut jeans, and his blue police shirt. Donna held his arm, teetering on the step below him. Dressed in dramatic white boots and a floral mini dress, she looked exactly like my Peace & Love Barbie doll.

"Nice dress," Dad complimented, admiring Donna's legs.

"You gonna let us in, Selbach, or just keep ogling my wife?" Greg joked.

"Mmmm smells good," Donna said, going down the hall to see if Lillian needed help.

Peter and I swarmed Donna, grabbing her waist as soon as she entered and sniffing the fruity scent that was her signature fragrance. Donna wore bright clothes, a year-round tan, and pale pink lipstick. Her long hair flipped up at the ends like the astronaut's wives in NASA news footage.

We played at the Deetham's house often. We were friends with freckle-faced Patty and mouthy Greg junior. But it was Donna we went to see. She filled the Deetham house with constant movement and music, dancing to celebrate the sun coming up in the morning and its setting at night. The Deetham house was a party of pink cocktails and endless fun.

Donna giggled at our clingy embrace. Kneeling, she asked, "So, Master Peter, how're you today?"

Peter blushed when Donna planted a perfect lipstick stain on his chubby cheek. "Yuck," he said, feigning embarrassment.

Donna let him go, trailing the sweet aroma of citrus as she headed to greet Lillian.

The two whispered for a moment, their backs to us so we could not hear.

"How's it been, Lillian? Any better?" Donna asked, her arm around Mom's shoulder.

"Same old. How about you?" Mom answered, stirring the pork gravy that simmered on the stove.

Donna lowered her dress from her shoulder to reveal a cantaloupe size bruise. "Rolling pin. Guess he didn't like the pie." Donna shrugged her shoulders before recovering the evidence.

"Oh God, Donna," was all Mom had managed before the men came up behind them, interrupting their sharing of miseries.

"Can a tall, handsome cop get a drink around here? Or is that jug of Gallo just for you ladies?" Greg appeared over Lillian and Donna. Donna's injured shoulder twitched.

"Sure thing. I'll pour for everyone." Donna spun on the square heel of her boot, filling the four glasses Mom had set on the counter.

Greg reached over Donna's shoulder to open the gallon-sized jug, pouring tippy-top portions for her and Lillian.

Dad took a sip. "To good meat and cute dresses." He clinked Greg's glass before leaving to check the roast.

"Here, here," Greg answered, laughing.

Donna and Lillian toasted with a light touch of glasses and nods. Donna downed half the glass on her first sip. The party had started.

Peter and I arrived, waiting on the bench closest to the sliding door. Dad delivered the sizzling meat to the banquet. All eyes lit at the gristly edges of the enormous entrée. Donna sat between Dad and Greg, filling her wine glass for the second time.

Mom brought the gravy boat and set it next to Mama's white serving bowl, which was filled with pickled red cabbage. "Say it," Dad instructed, looking at me. Despite his loathing of prayers, he gave in, and Mom would not eat unless we said the ridiculous thing.

"God is good. God is great. Thank you for our food. Amen," I recited, as anxious as my father to start eating.

He sliced the roast in perfect form, doling out slices to each plate. Donna picked at her food, more interested in the wine. I helped Peter cut his pork before eating. The sound of silverware and chewing usurped conversation until Peter spoke. "I can ride bikes with the big kids now. I got a two-wheeler," he told Donna excitedly, his mouth full of food.

Dad's reaction was as swift as a hatchet to the torso and just as shocking. He stood, pointing at Peter with the tip of his steak knife. "How many times have I told you not to talk with your mouth full?"

All eyes were on Dad. Peter trembled, tears forming at the corners of his brown eyes but not falling. Peter tried hard not to cry in front of him, saving his hurt for my embrace after the battle. After every beating, Mom begged him to cry. Daddy was never satisfied or done until he did.

"Say something, you idiot. For God's sake, do something with your boy, Lillian."

Donna downed her wine, "Time for refills," she said, leaving the porch with her glass. Greg kept eating, unaffected by Dad's dark tone or Peter's upset state.

"He's okay, Joe. Sit down," Lillian assured, trying to keep the peace for our guests.

"He's not okay. Who're you telling? I decide if he's okay, and he ain't fuckin okay," he roared. Standing to grab his side of the picnic table, he heaved it towards us. The food slid off in great heaps and crashes. Greg looked up, his fork frozen in the air.

Greg clucked his tongue, realizing he would not get more of the pork roast, which lay strewn across the cement floor. Swatting crumbs from his lap, he got up to join Donna inside.

The heavy wood landed hard on the top of Mom's thighs. She could not stand nor speak for the pain. Peter sobbed. I grew vengeful and furious that he had upset the meal, especially in front of the Deethams.

Dad righted the picnic table, eying the meal on the floor.

Glaring at Mom, I tried to calm Peter. "It's okay. Get cleaned up. I'll bring some food to your room."

Mom rubbed the aching pain in her legs, "Oh my God. It hurts," she whispered.

As I stooped to gather pork slices from the cement, Dad exploded, saying, "You think that hurts; that's nothing. I'll show you pain." Balling his hand, he leaned across to Mom, swinging hard, he landed a blow on her chin. He slammed out the door to the yard, shaking the semi-attached aluminum walls of the screen patio.

The Deethams returned to the porch, and Donna carried a towel filled with pontoon-shaped ice cubes from the ice maker. She placed the ice pack in Mom's lap. "Thank you," Mom said, bringing the ice to her chin before laying it across her thighs.

Donna and I tidied the patio in short order. All signs of the attack were erased except a trail of grease stains where the nub of the pork roast had bounced across the cement floor.

The temperature dropped. Donna urged us from the porch to the den. I foraged in the pantry for peanut butter, slathering it between two slices of Wonder Bread for my brother.

Listening for Daddy's return, I sat on the edge of my brother's bed. Peeling ends from the bread, I handed him the sloppy sandwich.

Peter wolfed it down. I answered an unspoken question, not realizing he had not asked it aloud. "Mr. Deetham went after him. Mrs. Deetham is with Mom. Just eat Peter. We'll play Go Fish when you finish."

He nodded, scooting across the floor to get the cards from the game basket at the bottom of his closet. I balled up the napkin he handed back after wiping his hands.

"Be right back. Throwing this away." Stopping to look at my reflection in the bathroom mirror, I tried to erase the weathering abuse from my expression. I looked older than my years. The shag haircut I begged for after seeing it on the cover of a *Teen Beat Magazine* framed my features severely. Turning sideways, I extended my belly, sighing at the chubby ugliness. Dropping the napkin in the trash, I returned to Peter, who had already dealt the cards.

"Do you have a five?" I asked.

"Go Fish."

We played for fifteen minutes before the slam of the front door reminded us of the ruined dinner. Within seconds, Dad appeared in the doorway. "Get in the kitchen. Help your mother with dessert." Like boot camp soldiers, we packed up the cards, obeying the order.

Mom was alone, slicing strawberries over the colander in the sink. "Dad said you need help?"

She looked up blankly. "Sure. Get the mixer; you can do the cream."

We loved mixer duty for the promise of a sweet ending. Mom always let us lick the leftover goodness from the beaters. Peter ran to the fridge to get the cream while I pulled a chair to the counter to reach the mixing bowl. Peter kneeled on the seat. Moving the handheld mixer too close to the edge of the glass bowl, he splattered cream on the backsplash. I took over, whipping the cream, sugar, and vanilla until peaks formed.

Lillian eyed the mixture, "I don't think that's enough. Run downstairs and grab the Cool Whip. We'll make the layers thin and leave the tub out if anyone wants more."

"Kay, Mom." I went to the dining room and opened the door to the basement, which squeaked like the devil's laughter. Tiptoeing down each step, I watched to see if Moonface glowed in the storage area. Moonface was the monster that lived in our basement, and he grew larger and more frightening with every family argument. His glow, fed by fear, frightened me every time I went down the builder-grade wood staircase.

My heart jumped when I reached the fifth step. Beside Moonface, something moved in the darkness. I prayed, "Please don't let it get me."

Finally, close enough to reach the light switch, I exhaled as I flipped it on, "Safe." When the back of the storage room came into focus, I backed up a step.

In the worn recliner, stored until Mom could get it reupholstered, sat my father, with Mrs. Deetham in his lap. Her boots were off; her flowered dress hitched high, exposing her panties. She was kissing Dad with her eyes closed.

I switched off the light as fast as I could, skipping steps on the way back up. I burst into the kitchen breathless. "Mom, you better get the whipped cream."

"What? Couldn't find it? Alright, you finish the strawberries."

Mom rushed downstairs as I watched. Flipping the switch, she turned the corner towards the freezer.

I knew she'd spotted Donna sitting in Dad's lap when she yelled, "What the hell? Your daughter saw you."

"Yeah, so what? She's old enough to see how adults act." I cringed at the confidence in his voice.

"Is it Joe? How about it, Donna? Is this how friends behave?" Her voice was shaky, and I imagined the glare Dad was giving her as Donna watched. They were two broken women, each obeying and regretting everything.

"Quit whining and get the damned dessert," Dad replied. "What yew gonna do now? Leave me? I'll kill you and the kids before you take two steps out the door."

I watched as Mom backed away from him, turning to head back up the stairs, wearing the dejected pose of defeat. I hid behind the door, waiting to see if Dad and Donna would follow.

I ran back to the kitchen before Mom reached my hiding spot, hoping she would reveal her anger. She did not. The corners of her mouth sagged as she stirred the whipped cream. To me, Dad's behavior was worthy of any flight risk. For Mom, fear seemed to be the barometer with which she measured every decision.

"Are we going? Should I pack?" I asked, hoping I might fan Dad's indiscretion into her last straw.

"What? No. Layer the sponge cake. I'm going to lie down. I have a headache."

Peter and I finished dessert duty. The basement door opened, followed by the front door. We stayed put, eating a slice and a half each of the sweet concoction while reflecting on the sourness of the day.

22 Lobster Races

Thick, black plastic covered the windows of my childhood home when the new owners purchased it after my father's death in 2015. The young couple thought it eerie that anyone would blacken windows to keep out the sun. They could not know that my father did not cover the windows to block the scenery nor that the blacked-out windows were a means for hiding.

Incursion irked my father to the bone. He did not like anyone looking at him without his invitation. He sought to control every angle and opinion of his life. When he wanted to impress strangers, he became a different man who smiled and engaged people in a sophisticated and somewhat appealing manner. He had mastered the art of getting what he wanted with the lies he told himself and others. A changeling, Dad wore many faces, most of them false.

When I was a child, the Medford home was a private place where physical violence and hurtful words lived, never to be spoken of outside. Dad disliked anything or anyone who might discover his transgressions, and a disposition of self-protection defined him.

Blacking out windows was just another way for my father to control how the world viewed his truth.

~ ~ ~

Hope raised its head in June, the budding month when leaves turn green and rabbits munch on clover-covered lawns. On the last day of sixth grade, I ran home.

"What's the hurry?" asked Kenny Anderson as I sped past my friend Laura's house.

"Lobster," I shouted despite being out of breath. "It's my favorite."

Slowing in front of our house, I caught my breath, sliding the bookbag from my shoulder to clutch it in my arms. The front door was open. "I'm home, Ma," I announced as I hurried down the hall to unpack my school things.

Dad inspected our rooms each night, ensuring the floors were clear of clothing and that shelved items stood in neat rows. Hanging my book bag on the hook inside my closet door, I inspected my room for any infractions Dad might notice. Satisfied there were none, I sock-slid down the wood floor of the hallway towards the kitchen. It was time for the lobster races.

Running live lobsters across the linoleum floor was an annual sport reserved for the last school day before summer vacation. It was a celebration Peter and I looked forward to all year. Dad called our ritual, "a sport for spoiled brats."

Before he met Mom, Dad's closest encounter with a crustacean was watching black-tie diners feast from a fifth-story construction site. Thanks to Mom's Uncle Sammie, the wealthiest and most connected of her father's five brothers, Mom ate lobster every year growing up.

The speckled blue pot simmered on the gas stove. Husked corn on the cob rested on the counter. Peter beat me to the race. He sat Indian style on the floor, poking a squirming crustacean with a spatula. The lobster, oblivious to its opportunity to bolt, meandered toward the carpeted den.

Mom smiled at us with her back to the stove. She wore her favorite purple polyester pants and matching sleeveless shirt. It was an outfit reserved for special occasions. She removed another lobster from the paper bag to place it on the floor.

She clapped lobster claw oven mitts together in soundless applause when Peter's contender revved up to crawl under the table. As my lobster sped up, the front door opened like a pause button. Even the lobsters seemed to sense Dad's arrival, suspending the slippery race.

To our collective relief, Dad went to the shower, and the room reanimated as if recovering from a game of freeze tag. The hiss of the boiling water and the sound of the shower offered a simultaneous whoosh. Mom leaned down to retrieve the weary lobsters and tossed them into the ice-filled sink.

Peter and I sat waiting for Dad to emerge squeaky clean for the killing. He arrived wearing the smile of a maniacal dentist. His grin widened as he dropped the lobsters one by one into the boil, lowering his ear to catch the final torture of his food. I covered my ears until the lobster's screaming ceased. Dropping the lid, he reminded us of his childhood deprivation, "We didn't get any damn lobster in my house, I'll tell yew. We ate eel. Yew should have seen dat thing squirm."

With his share of the dinner preparation complete, Dad sat at his feeding throne while Mom delivered the bright red sea bugs to our plates. Wearing plastic bibs decorated with cartoon lobsters, we broke claws with metal tongs, dipping the treasured insides into melted butter. Dad feasted with an intensity born of his German roots, crushing claws with his bare hands. Lifting a chunk of dripping white flesh to his mouth, he paused mid-bite when the doorbell rang.

"Uh-oh," I pulled the sweet corn cob from my buttery lips. "Hope it's not one of my friends," I whispered into my lap, thinking it unlikely since everyone knew our house was off-limits at dinner time. Dad did

147

not like visitors, doorbells, or anything else to interrupt his nighttime meal.

Lowering the silver pick he used to dig meat from spiny crevices, he glared at each of us before leaving the table to answer the door.

The sound of a small, whiny voice reached us, "Good evening, sir. My name is Bob, and I have a fantastic Amway special to tell you about. Is the missus at home?"

Dad's voice rumbled, "What do you want wid my wife?"

"Well, sir, our products…" the salesmen answered in a joyful tone.

The vibration of the slamming door toppled a pile of shells on the newspaper-covered table. Dad returned; his appearance mutated from king of the castle to crimson devil. The color of his clean-shaven skin now matched our boiled dinner. We watched him pull a fresh bib from the pack with his pinkies extended. Tying it around his neck, he re-commenced eating. Mom sipped Chianti from a five-gallon jug that cost $5.95 at Pathmark, pouring a third glass when the doorbell sounded again.

I reached under the table to hold Peter's sticky hand without Dad seeing. Dad stopped chewing, wiped butter from his pursed lips, and returned to the front door.

Looking at us with an expression that suggested surrender, Mom downed the entire glass of wine.

"Sir, I just wanted to leave a brochure," The salesman's voice faded, and a great swoosh and rattle took its place.

"What, what, what?" the salesman-turned-parrot shrieked.

Unable to resist, I tip-toed down the hall in time to see Dad's fist meet the Amway rep's cheek. Like a slow-motion scene from a Saturday morning cartoon, the salesman's eyeglasses took flight over the front stoop. He wore a stunned expression that scared me back to the kitchen.

The door slammed shut, and Dad returned, embers burning in his blue eyes. Mom, unable to see the tipping point that was obvious to me, asked in her relaxed-by-wine voice, "Did you get a brochure, Joe? I love Amway."

I grabbed Peter's hand in relay speed to retreat to the den. Volcanic ash arose, and lava followed. I turned on the TV with the volume low. The console lit up halfway through an episode of *Happy Days*.

The Fonz crooned, "Ayyyee!"

Mom said, "Oooohhhh," and the vowel-engorged battle began.

Dad grabbed her throat. She struggled to say something as lobster parts flew like confused falcons.

The doorbell chimed again. Dad released Mom. She bled from a gash on her head, the revenge of a lifeless lobster claw now wedged in the radiator. As the front door opened again, I wiped my mother's bleeding head with a damp towel.

"Sir, I'm pressing charges. You can't attack…"

"My goddamn dinner…" is all we heard before the screen door wheezed shut. The sitcom ended with a tuneful promise: "These happy days are yours and mine, happy days."

"I hope so," I rolled my eyes, patting Mom's head and listening for sirens.

The police offered Dad the usual cuff and duck routine as we watched from behind the screen door.

"What do you have to say for yourself this time, Selbach?" a rotund police officer asked.

Dad growled, "He interrupted my lobster dinner. Do yew have any idea how much that shit costs?"

Neighbors lit porch lights in rapid succession. Filtering out into the night, they peered at the front of our house. With Peter clinging to my waist, I stepped on the front stoop to get a better look at the object of the neighbor's intense focus. My jaw dropped.

The Amway salesman hung suspended by the back of his pant belt from the iron flagpole attached to our house. His black sample case rested on the lawn below his feet. He was a flailing mess of weak bellowing as he waved an accusatory finger toward the police car. Someone unhooked him from the pole. Dad sat in the cruiser for a long time while Mom talked to the police, defending him. An officer escorted the bruised and mortified salesman to the end of the driveway. His eyes cast downward, I watched him shake his head, and I knew he would not press charges.

After the porch lights darkened and emergency vehicles departed, I tucked Peter into bed. As the adults discussed the incident outside, I tidied up the kitchen, removing lobster parts from the silverware drawer, sink, and ceiling. On my knees, I used the dustpan to scoop up crustaceous leftovers. As I deposited the debris of the last day of school celebration in the trash, I picked up a claw to suck out the last luscious meat from it.

Summer had arrived dangerously.

23 Target Practice

Sheltering and shuttling children from harm, parents wield divine power in their ability to protect.

My father held his power to impress outsiders higher than our safety. Yet, I loved him.

I hate that I loved a man who thought himself more precious than the children he adopted or the woman he promised to love. I sometimes wonder if the duality of loving and hating Dad is a sign that I have Stockholm Syndrome. How am I still psychologically bonded to the man who held us hostage all those years?

My father's brother, Karl, does not believe my father raged because she was transgender. He believes that mental illness was the root of Dad's behavior. I think that mental illness and hiding were twin monsters in the birthing of our misery.

~ ~ ~

It was the week after the lobster boil, and while still in our pajamas, Peter and I teased and tormented each other with affectionate toy drama. My brother slammed his Tonka tractor into a bridge of thirty-two wooden blocks. I propped up Barbie next to GI Joe in the dream house, a gift from Santa the year before. The exposed cement walls of the basement offered a chilled respite from the record-breaking heat of that summer. The raw-edged throw rug was our playtime island, the one place where we could act like kids.

"Ewww," Peter exclaimed when I bent Barbie's head to kiss GI Joe in the plastic living room.

I giggled at his disgust, making smooching sounds to go with the scene. Peter grabbed his GI Joe and set him atop the truck, making shooting sounds. "Pew, pew, pew." He toppled the rest of the blocks in a scattering of delight.

Our giggling role play halted when Dad hollered down the stairs, "Breakfast. Get washed up. Now."

Sunday was bagel day. We hurried to stow the blocks and toys. Upstairs, paper plates, butter, cream cheese, sliced onions and tomatoes, and smoked lox waited. As soon as Mom joined us, we dug into the paper sack, choosing from the baker's dozen of poppy, everything, onion, and salt bagels. Mom sliced the doughy goodness, setting aside half an everything bagel for herself.

"That all you gonna eat?" Dad reprimanded. "Yew lose weight, and I have to buy you more clothes. That shit costs money." He nodded, rubbing his ample stomach.

Mom added the other half to her plate and slathered on the fixings. Dad seemed pleased.

Sunday bagels were a ritual of truce, a peaceful chomping and slurping of orange juice that begat normalcy. Under the baked goodness of that morning lurked a plan that would turn stomachs sour and brew an amplified level of mistrust.

Our stomachs stretched beyond another bagel bite; we started to settle in front of the television. Dad stopped us. "Get dressed, we got something to do."

We got dressed, meeting Dad in the driveway. "Come on, get in," Dad ordered.

Peter looked at me, questioning. "Where we going, Dad?" I asked.

"To the loon's. Hear she's acting up," Dad answered.

A few blocks from the Selbach abode lived a woman whose dingy yard was the eyesore of the development. Overgrown and cluttered with a discarded couch and bags of garbage, her yard was the picture of crazy. Dad called her *the loon* because, "Anyone who lets their yard turn to that kind of shit has to be nuts."

The loon liked to watch people pass her house. She stared at every person and vehicle that passed her three-paneled picture window. I had never seen her in person. She was just a shadowy figure lurking and looking out her front window. I figured she was just old and lonely. But some of the kids in the neighborhood said she was crazy, which made running, rather than walking, past her house an unspoken rule— never walk, always run, the crazy lady was looking.

That morning, Dad herded us into the Maverick and drove us slowly past the loon's house. A few folks had gathered on the sidewalk across the street, and Dad parked a few houses away. We got out of the car, and Dad coaxed us towards the curiosity.

"Did you hear?" a big wheel rider with bright red hair and freckles squealed. "Crazy lady is pointing a gun out."

We walked up the block toward the straggle of interested residents. The group, dressed in an array of seventies casual wear, had stopped just short of the old lady's property. Across the street, to the left and right of the house, bees buzzed along with curious neighbors. I touched Peter's back, relieved that, for once, we were not the focus of the fuss.

Holding Peter's hand tight, I watched Dad for signs of doom. His hands opened and closed, and he appeared to expand, puffing up as he pushed toward the yard.

Dad nudged us ahead of him. Lowering his head to my ear, he whispered, "Walk."

I looked up, confused, "What?"

He shoved us forward again, "Walk." Our father had decided to test the loon's insanity with our lives.

"No, Dad, I don't want to," I insisted, trying to pull Peter in the opposite direction.

"Take your brother and go," Dad ordered.

More afraid of Dad than dodging a crazy lady's bullet, I held Peter closer, starting across the old ladies' stretch of sidewalk. A click-clack of awe rose from the bystanders.

Before we had traveled four steps, Dad instructed, "Don't you dare run."

I positioned Peter on the outside closest to the street. Blocking him as best I could, I held his hand, squeezed it to reassure him, and started our journey past the house.

The beating of my heart constricted my throat. We walked ten steps, and I could feel the loon's stare. I heard a bicycle kickstand scrape the sidewalk as we reached the middle of her property. A woman with rollers in her hair gasped, and we ducked, walking faster.

"Slow down," Dad belched from the safety of the sidewalk.

When we finally reached the other side of the loon's property, a woman wearing a strawberry-embroidered apron hugged us. Looking like she had watched a thief steal from a charity jug, she glared at Dad, who strolled past the loon's house after us.

"Does my face look funny?" I asked the aproned lady, feeling the heat of the melt bubbling up on my cheeks.

"No, dear, you're okay. My God, you're all right." She hugged me harder.

The loon lowered the gun from the window, retreating into the darkened room. It was the first time in years that she did not peer from that window. Relieved laughter mingled with a chatter of disbelief. "That coulda been a tragedy," a neighbor said, shaking her head, "Not sure who's crazier, that guy or her."

A man in plaid shorts shook Dad's hand, clearly impressed. Dad shook back, crushing the well-wisher's fingers with his confidence.

As the small group dispersed, the sound of a single police siren entered the development. Only a couple of neighborhood kids remained when the cop pulled into the loon's driveway.

In the back of the car on the way home, Peter retreated into himself. I stared at the back of my dad's head, wishing it would explode in a gory horror-film ending.

I found my voice, "Why'd you make us do that, Dad? She could've shot us?"

"She wouldn't. The old bat's a pushover."

"But we could've been killed." I choked back tears at the idea of a bullet hitting my baby brother.

"Calm the fuck down. She didn't shoot you. For God's sake, you kids are so dramatic."

As we approached the house, I spotted Mom on the front stoop. She was wringing her hands. Dad had taken us for our *drive* while she was in the bathroom. She hurried to the back door of the Maverick. "Are you okay?" she asked.

Peter and I nodded.

Dad got out of the driver's seat, bursting with the news, "You shoulda seen it, Lillian. Jean stopped by this morning. That crazy lady a few blocks over had a gun pointed out her front window. Looked like she broke a pane of the bay window. Gonna cost her. That shit's expensive. I knew the bitch wasn't gonna shoot. Sent the kids across her property, and she didn't do shit. That woman's fucking nuts."

Mom's jaw dropped. "You forced the kids to walk in front of her house? When she had a gun?" She looked at us in the back seat. "Stay in the car. We're going grocery shopping."

155

Peter snuggled close to me. Dad walked to the mailbox to chat with Jean, who'd pulled up as we spoke to Mom. Dad took up an imaginary gun, pointing it toward the car.

Backing down the driveway, Mom rolled down the window, "Going to Pathmark. Need a few things for dinner." Dad waved her away like a mosquito.

Speeding down the street in the Maverick, Mom stopped at the Route 112 intersection. She stared at the heavy traffic, sitting at the stop sign too long.

"Mom, I'm going to the city with Peter if you don't leave Dad," I announced from the back seat.

Mom turned, tears streaming down her cheeks, "I'm sorry," she sobbed. "He promised...; I don't even have a high school diploma. How am I going to support us? I never even had a real job."

I could not hear my mother's excuse-making. I did not care about money, and my escape plan proved it. I had rehearsed everything in my mind but wondered if the plan would work. Finally revealing the plan to my mother, the words bubbled in a massive rush, "I hate him. Peter hates him. I'm leaving. Last time we went to the Bronx Zoo, I saw people living in boxes. I'm gonna make one, a real nice one. It'll have cutout windows, curtains, everything." I traced a square in the air. Lowering my hands, I continued, "Peter and I'll live there. I saved my allowance for food and train tickets. We have to go before he kills us. We have to go now."

Mom sobbed. Her shoulders heaved with each intake of breath. "What have I done?"

I watched out the car window as a toddler skipped from the McDonald's restaurant. Her father caught her in his arms before she crossed the parking lot. Mom drove down Route 112 towards the Pathmark grocery store.

Considering the groceries we would need, and convinced Mom would buy them, I asked, "Can we get canned stuff, Mom? We won't have a fridge."

The minute we stepped from the car, Mom gathered us in a suffocating powwow. "I'm gonna make it right. I'll get my GED. I have to do something. I'll make this right; I swear." After seventeen years of marriage, she had finally reached her limit. Her body pulsed with the possibility of freedom.

We searched the bulletin board near the cash registers. The cork board was littered with advertisements for cleaning services, accountants, and household goods. Mom was looking for a flier she had seen many times before. She found it under an index card advertising a used stove. "Battered, need help. Call Safe Haven. 1-800-555-5555."

My stomach burned with hope as she wrote down the number. "We're gonna be okay, Peter," I assured my silent brother. "You see that sign. It says we're gonna be safe." Peter stood a bit taller, emerging from the faraway place where he often retreated.

Mom deposited a dime in a pay phone near the produce section. I rubbed Peter's hands together as the AC and refrigeration iced the air.

"Hello," Mom's voice cracked. "We need help."

A few shoppers slowed to watch our crestfallen trio. Mom whispered, covering the mouthpiece with a cupped hand. We clung together, our arms and legs intertwined.

"What are you looking at?" I asked a sharp-nosed grocery clerk whose spectacles hung low, exposing his nosiness. He had stopped sorting fruit to watch us. Huffing, he pushed his glasses back into place, inspecting each apple in the green pyramid for bruises.

Mom pulled a receipt from her purse. Digging in the zipper compartment for a pen, she scribbled an address on the crinkled paper. "Thank you. I will. Yes. Goodbye." She hung up the phone.

Mom wrapped her arms around us. "We're leaving on Monday as soon as Dad goes to work. I promise."

Mom had sworn the same promise five other times, and I believed her the first three times. Every bold proclamation seemed genuine, and I think Mom meant it every time she said we'd leave. But, somehow, we never did. Her fear sent us back to unsafe beds to dream the same bad dreams that had defined our childhood. I reacted to Mom's promise with a dull ache of optimism. Untangling myself from the huddle, I said, "Sure hope so, Mom."

Mom recognized the disbelief in my voice and reached to pull me back to her.

"We need milk," I said, shrugging away the painful hope of the embrace.

24 Exhale

Knowing what you want and getting it are two terribly different things.

Shooting Dad might have been easier than watching him leave and spending the next three months wondering when he'd be back to kill us.

~ ~ ~

Two days after the loon incident, I watched as Dad backed his truck down the driveway. Half convinced that we would leave, I whispered against the glass, "Bye, Dad." My breath fogged the pane. Putting my finger on the wet surface, I traced a sad face as it faded.

With my cheek resting against the glass, I recalled how the stubble of my father's cheek felt as we danced to Al Martino's "Daddy's Little Girl." It was my favorite memory, one I had turned into a destination to visit in moments whenever fear loomed and I needed something bigger to believe in.

I had discovered the song years before while riding in my mother's car. When the song came on the AM radio, its dreamy crescendos and plodding beat opened a vein of hope. The song's sentiment proved that some Dads treasured their daughters.

The next time I heard the song was at a family wedding, where it revealed my father's soft interior life. Like the prince in Disney's *Cinderella,* he lifted me into his arms. In a slow spin, my feet dangled above the floor. He mouthed the words without sound. All that I dreamed of spilled silently from his lips. I was his treasure and deserved holding. I was sugar and spice. I was loved, and he thought me nice.

Dad's dewdrop eyes and relaxed jaw perplexed and thrilled me that night. Coddled, warm, and finally adored, I squeezed his broad shoulders. It was a feeling I would spend a lifetime trying to recapture. Watching him drive away that morning, I mourned dances that would never come and the Dad who could never love me more than himself.

Conflicted between regret and celebration, I watched a squirrel pounce on an acorn at the center of the pristine lawn. It looked up, wobbling to keep hold of the treat, as Dad's truck rumbled down the road.

Mom opened her bedroom door a minute later. "Pack enough clothes for one week. Then help Peter. We have to be at the diner by ten."

"We're going, Mom?" I didn't believe her. We had been apart from my father just once. I was ten when, in the heat of a battle, Mom told him to go away. To Peter's and my delighted amazement, he did.

He left us for two blissful months, during which I got my first taste of what it meant to be a kid. Friends, Susan and Laura, slept over at my house, and I stayed up late, left my clothes bunched on the floor, and slept worry-free. It was our happiest time in Medford.

However, that freedom flew away on downtrodden wings once Mom could not pay the mortgage. She called the state welfare office which said they could not help her. The system was set up to help renters in low-income housing, and house owners need not apply. Without a high school diploma or a job, Mom believed she was stuck. She called Dad. The devil returned, his rage refueled by the respite.

I danced a little jig when Mom said we were leaving that morning. She smiled for a half moment. "Go, we have a half hour. Bring a couple of toys. Not too much. We'll be in one room at the shelter."

I dumped a Barbie bathing suit and wedding gown once swapped for two polyester pantsuits to the floor. I'd won the outfits trading with Laura down the street. It was a weekly ritual that assured fashion variety for our beloved dolls. Grabbing a wad of tiny garments from the vinyl case, I tossed them into the air. They littered the carpet, some reaching my unmade bed. I giggled at the prospect of leaving them there. "Take that, Dad," I huffed, choosing two Barbies for the trip.

Tucking nightgowns, shirts, pants, and my favorite sundress in the pink suitcase, I sat for a while, flipping through the record albums stacked at the foot of my bed. Andy Gibb smiled from a cover, and I wondered if I was too young to marry him. Choosing four of my favorites, I carried them to the hall along with my portable record player.

I opened my brother's door to find him sitting in bed, his brow permanently singed into the worried furrow that hurt my stomach. He gazed at me from the charmed state between dreaming and panic. In his arms lay Chugga, his beloved stuffed puppy. Peter twisted the broken strap of Chugga's train conductor overalls, blinking sleepily.

"We're leaving," I told him, hunting under his bed for the bag he had used to stow baseball equipment until Dad punched the little league coach during a home game. Dad stormed from the wooden bleachers after the coach called out to my brother in the outfield, "Look lively, Selbach." The seasoned coach, distinguished for his good sportsmanship and quick smile, filed assault charges against Dad, dropping them later. Peter never played baseball again.

"Where we going?" he yawned, dropping Chugga to stretch his arms overhead.

"Someplace safe," I answered, finding the bag and dumping its contents on the floor.

"Dad's gonna be mad," Peter said, looking at the mess.

"I don't care. Help me get your clothes packed. Then get dressed."

Peter gave up the warmth of his bed to help me stuff his belongings into the bag. Taking Chugga from my brother's lap, I squashed the stuffed toy in. Together, we tugged at the zipper, barely closing the duffle.

Peter smiled a rare toothy grin, "Where we going?"

"Remember we talked about our nest. Kinda like that, but Mom's going with us. You can bring a truck and a couple of Matchbox cars too. Put them on top of the bag. Not too many. Mom says we'll be in one room."

"I'm not sleeping in a room with you," Peter bickered without conviction.

"Okay. Just get ready." I left him to get dressed, rushing down the hall. Mom's suitcases were at the spot where the hallway split to the front door. They were the same cases we used on the cruise to Bermuda, a happy memory, except for Dad's altercation with the parent of a kid who playfully lifted Peter close to the railing. A ship employee had to steer Dad away from the man, saving him and our five-day vacation.

I paused in the hall, unable to look away from the killing closet. I would miss my hiding place, but not the premeditation that drove me there.

I wondered if we should take Dad's shotgun with us to the shelter. *Would he use it on someone when he found us gone? Would he hurt a neighborhood pet to vent his anger?* He'd done it before. The police came that time. Peter, Mom, and I watched them talk to Dad through the screened door. Dad invited the officers in, and my heart beat fast with the expectation of his arrest. I needed someone to take my father away.

The idea of peace was an unwieldy marlin, difficult to catch, but precious. If the police took him, the struggles and the bloodletting would fade, leaving our trophy intact. Peter and I waited behind my father as they questioned him. I held my hands behind my back, crossing my fingers for luck.

"We have a report of shots fired," the lanky officer said, touching his holstered weapon.

"You shoot at the neighbor's dog, Selbach?" asked the other, tapping at the handcuffs on his belt.

"What do you think?" Dad scoffed, seeming to grow taller in the presence of the police. A fearless bull, he snorted at their questions.

I nodded, thinking how I'd like to be fearless someday. The cuff-ready cop noticed. I liked the cop's slowness and eyes which seemed to search for my truth. He would not find our truth there. I had been waltzing this dangerous dance for years, learning to be silent after the first cop had left us standing open-mouthed in the hall.

Dad swung his entire body around to see what had captured the officer's attention. I hung my head. Peter dug his face into Mom's side. Dad was a peacock, strutting at the invisibility the system allowed him. Watching their interaction was exhausting, like trying to pull my weight up the long rope suspended from the ceiling in PE class. My small arms remained at my sides, weak and ineffective.

"Mr. Selbach, this ain't the first time your neighbors have called us about you." I looked up, recognizing the pimple-faced policeman from the time I dared call the police on my father. He had punched Mom in the stomach for saying she wanted to take night classes to get her high school diploma.

"So, what?" Dad stared us down as he spoke to the cops. "No one pressed any goddamn charges. They ain't gonna this time either."

He was right. Mom never pressed charges. Before the police arrived, Dad threatened to kill the first one of us who spoke. A volcano cannot hold back its ash forever, yet somehow, I faced that police officer, doing just that. I held my tongue, praying he'd notice the thick makeup around Mom's eye. *Why are adults so dumb?* I pondered; *can't you see he'll kill us if we tell you the truth?* I had long since put aside the useful police images sold on *Sesame Street* and *Mr. Rogers*. Another curiously empty untruth sold by adults.

On the day of our real escape, I passed the killing closet, touching the thin wood that housed my dark visions of murder. I found Mom standing at the center of the kitchen, looking at the custom cabinets and chosen appliances. Like an Etch A Sketch, she shook her head, clearing the lost look from her eyes. "Get a few snacks for the ride, okay?"

I opened the well-stocked pantry, filling a paper sack with pop tarts and cookies.

"Put in some canned food. I don't know if the shelter will have food." I tucked in two cans of SpaghettiOs.

"I," Mom stuttered. "Bring the allowance you saved. I'll pay you back if we have to spend it."

"Okay." I had tucked the money away for a different kind of escape, hiding it in my ballerina jewelry box under a cardboard canister of Tinker Toys at the back of my closet.

After gathering all the coins we could find under couch cushions, in coat pockets, and from our piggy banks, we held hands under the hall light. Peter looked from me to Mom. We all gaped at the small pile of items gathered between us. We did not speak as we carried our cases to the car. Mom packed the trunk so full we had to lean on it to get it to latch.

My portable record player, a box of important papers, and the pearl inlay crucifix that Papa gave Mom as a child filled the front passenger seat. The cross had saved my father's life, and I took it with me for the hope it represented. I hoped we would never hang it back on the Medford wall and that it would protect us wherever we landed.

I did not look back as we pulled away from the house. Wherever we were going would be safer. A gaggle of stork-legged teens held a fundraiser carwash, and I envied their happy faces and secure lives. We drove through a dozen stoplights. My mother went into the chrome diner alone. A big-haired lady wearing thick glasses and a sad smile handed her a piece of paper.

Mom put the paper with the directions to our destination atop the cross. We started the journey following the signs to Montauk, a beach community defined by dunes, crabgrass, and shingled sea huts.

A silent twenty minutes later, Mom opened the window. A whiff of iodine-soaked air wafted through the car. I cranked the back window, sticking my head out to inhale the briny seaweed. Licking my lips, I took a deep breath. "The air tastes like salt, Peter. Stick out your tongue."

Peter licked at the air. "I don't taste it. Pew. This place stinks."

"That's the ocean," Mom reminded. "You'll have so much fun at the beach, and you can ride the waves."

A dozen weathered wood fences lined the road. The car bounced on potholes born of the weathering effect of sea and sand. Mom glanced at the directions periodically to find our destination. We spotted snippets of beach between the houses and craggy elevations, and a hopeful elation settled in. "Look at that one. I'm gonna jump in as soon as we get there." Peter pointed at the colliding waves.

The pebbled asphalt on the road to the motel ended, and we rode the last half mile on dirt. An overgrown hedge hid the entrance until we were almost past it. A rusty metal sign indicated, "Parking for guests only." Just a few cars inhabited the lot. We looked for the office, finding it where a half-lit *Office* sign fizzled on and off in the window.

The rundown motel tucked away in Southampton sheltered us that night and for sixty-two more.

That first evening huddled on the scratchy sheets of the lumpy bed, we watched sitcom reruns on a ten-inch black-and-white television, along with news of the big bicentennial celebration in New York City. A threadbare throw rug and mildew-coated window shade decorated our temporary abode. It was a hell hole. But the devil in Medford had no idea where it was, which cast it as a heavenly respite.

A family with two, three, or four members lived in each of the twenty motel rooms. Patsy was the one childless resident. Allowed because of her grave injuries, Patsy wore long sleeves and pants in the blistering heat. She pulled at her cuffs, apologizing as she tried to hide the burns that had been inflicted on her by her boyfriend.

The shelter's residents wore their wounds inside and out. One child named Charlie smacked his own cheek every few minutes, as if testing to see if he was still alive. No matter their path to the shelter, residents shared a state of fear mixed with budding freedom. Most came from suburban homes with bright kitchens, large playrooms, and green landscapes. They were African American, White, Hispanic, and Asian. As we discovered that summer, abusers do not discriminate.

Counselors crammed each day with activities for the younger children. Coloring contests and trips to the playground transformed fright into careful laughter. Lifting the spirits of broken children was the task of shelter volunteers. They undertook each sorrowful case with the same gentle touch one might use to mend the broken wing of a sparrow. Despite missing the yellow Tonka trucks and treasured storybooks of home, Peter emerged, giggling in his newfound safety.

I was the oldest motel child. In the dirt parking lot, the younger kids played kickball and jumped rope, kicking up clouds of dust and laughing as only the recently freed can. I liked watching them, seeing past black eyes to the giddiness of being free. However, I had no time for the trivialities of childhood. At nearly thirteen, I was too old for the games. My heart was weighed down with the burden of homelessness. I had a hard time escaping the worry of what came next. So, I filled the unstructured days watching sitcoms, listening to my Bee Gees albums, and standing guard.

Summer eked on in a scorching humdrum, the afternoon sun punishing my protective nature. It beat down on the roofless porch, where I watched for my father. Careful not to touch the heated arms of the rusted metal chair outside our motel room, I planned for my dad's arrival. With a stack of rocks at my feet for throwing and a plaid bowtie—found on the floor of the motel laundry—for choking, I waited, terrified that he would find us.

Time moved stubbornly; minutes ticked along with my heartbeat, turning to hours. As the young woman approached, I kicked at the sandy gravel, tasting a salty trickle of fear on my lip. Sliding the chair from our neighbor Christine's room—who never ventured outside due to a healing collarbone, broken ankle, and other wounds Mom said I shouldn't ask about—the woman sat next to me. Shading her eyes from the sun, she stared at my small collection of rocks and down the gravel drive.

"Hi," she said, "I'm Lisa. What'cha looking for?"

I eyed the pretty, dark-haired woman with cautious curiosity. "Just making sure," I answered, choosing my words carefully. I had to be courteous and not say anything that might get us kicked out of the shelter. We had no place else to go.

"Where are Mom and Peter?" Lisa asked.

Anxious, I thought the woman was about to tell me that the monster had grabbed them. "Mom's taking her GED class. Peter went to the playground with the other kids."

A cloud of dust rose from a passing car, and I shuddered at the idea of being left at the shelter alone. "They're okay, right?"

167

Lisa smiled a genuine smile that relaxed me. Putting her hand on mine, she assured me, "They're fine. You're safe now. I want to talk in the office for a bit. It's awful hot out here."

"Yeah, I guess." I licked my lips again. I was dying of thirst and bored.

I followed Lisa to the makeshift office, where she offered me a cola which I drank too fast. I burped noisily, "I'm sorry."

Lisa laughed, and I smiled, looking around the office. The only furniture beside our chairs was a metal desk and three file cabinets covered by plastic bins full of welfare and education forms. An air conditioner whirred in the window, and it was much newer than the one in our room.

"Nice and cold in here," I said, tipping back the metal folding chair.

"Yes, it is. I notice you sit in the parking lot every day. Don't you have anything else you'd like to do?"

"Not really, plus…" I stopped, not wanting to imply anything bad about the place where she worked.

"I understand why you do it. But I want you to remember that the location of our shelter is kept secret. Your father won't find you here, and none of the bad men who hurt the residents can find this place." Lisa looked serious.

I wanted to believe her, but Mom had assured me of our safety too many times before. "He won't do it again. He's getting better. I think he's trying." I had heard it all. I just nodded.

Lisa frowned, realizing it would not be easy to convince me. "I can tell you don't trust me. But none of the men have found us yet, right?" Her warm voice was calm, unrushed.

"Yeah, but how long has this place been here? For people like us?"

"Six months. Not bad, right?"

"Yeah, I guess."

"Your Mom did the right thing. You're safe here."

Lisa's open expression made me feel like we were friends. She acted like she might understand how running from an impossible home into an impossible predicament felt.

We met every day after that to talk about abuse and opportunities. "Your Mom will get a great job when you leave. She's going to have her high school diploma," she said. "She might even go to college. Do you want to go to college?"

I shrugged, "No idea. Haven't thought about it."

"Well, you should. I've been a volunteer here for a year, and I've seen some smart kids. You're bright. Any idea what you want to do when you grow up?

"Well, I like to listen to albums. I have three, kinda boring. I might be a singer or an actress." Worried Lisa would ask me to sing, I added, "I also read a lot. I read all the paperbacks from the laundry."

"You like reading?" she asked brightly. "Guess we'll have to find you more books." Lisa smiled, "You won't be here forever. You know things are going to get better, right?"

"Sure," I said without conviction. Leaving the motel was almost as frightening as the idea of Dad finding us.

"You're strong," Lisa enforced. "You should be proud of how well you cared for your family."

"How'd you find out about that?"

"Well, I interviewed your mother at intake when you arrived. She told me how brave you were and that you were always getting in between your Dad and her."

"Yeah, I guess." A car pulled into the parking area, and I looked, "I hate him."

"It's okay to feel that way. It's okay, Vicki."

169

Lisa listened to me talk about my father for an hour. Her encouragement and rosy demeanor felt like an unexpected hug. So, I started going to her office every afternoon.

On the sixteenth day after we met, I plopped down on Lisa's couch to enjoy the air-conditioning. "I have something for you," she smiled.

I sat up, holding out my hand as she handed me a worn paperback she pulled from her purse. A somber woman wearing a bonnet and gown stared from the cover.

"It is *Jane Eyre*. You'll like it better than those romance novels from the laundry."

I flipped through the first pages. Minuscule print and more words than I had ever read in a single book made the idea of reading it daunting. Trusting Lisa and not wanting to seem ungrateful, I said, "Thanks."

I read *Jane Eyre* every night after that. I also read it during my afternoon watches, which morphed from dreadful to hopeful as I awaited Lisa's arrival each day.

As I delighted in every precious page of my newfound heroine's story, Peter grew an inch in courage and height. Mom earned her high-school diploma. The dynamic of our relationships changed. No longer targets in a duck shoot, we discovered the calm of being a family.

"What kind of job?" I asked Mom one night as we snuggled in the shared full-size bed.

"Not sure. They're looking for the right one."

The window AC sputtered, and we looked at each other.

"Uh-oh." Peter flipped over, throwing an arm over his eyes so he would not have to look at the dying source of cold air. Once it shuddered back to circulation, the conversation resumed.

"How soon do we have to leave?" I asked.

"Two more weeks, then they get us an apartment. In Patchogue, I think."

"That's close to Dad," Peter whined, sounding frightened.

"He's okay with it," Mom said. "He gets the house."

"Why don't we get it? There are three of us, and he's all alone."

"Because I can't afford it." She swatted a fly away, and I cringed. Mom frowned. "I had to let him have the house so he'd agree to the divorce."

A volunteer lawyer filed the separation papers on Mom's behalf. Dad's written response was uncharacteristically smooth. He would keep everything in exchange for an uncontested divorce. The lawyer warned Mom, "You can fight for your belongings, but I advise against it. You ended up here because he is a dangerous man. Freedom is expensive but worth it."

Mom agreed to Dad's conditions.

"What about our toys? I forgot my red baseball cap." Peter asked as Mom tried to explain our father's selfish decision to keep everything.

"We'll get some of it. I'll figure it out." Mom rubbed her forehead like she had every time Dad came home.

I frowned. "Patchogue schools? Will I be with my friends?"

"I'm not sure." Mom scratched all over as if our questions were a rash.

"We'll be okay. That's what matters, right?" Mom asked, not expecting an answer. "Now go to sleep; we're going to the movies in the morning."

I turned from Mom, making a mental list of the things I would never have again. Like *Jane Eyre*, I was learning how much I had to lose *and gain* from fleeing our oppressor.

25 Independence Day

Our escape, floating outside the normalcy of having a home and unhooked from hateful days, was so surreal that I close my eyes when I think of it. Being homeless in the Hamptons was a beautiful irony. We were safe but penniless, hidden but outsiders. We wore the few middle-class fashions we'd shoved in our suitcases on the escape day while designer-clad darlings drove by in Benzes and Bugattis.

For anyone unfamiliar with the Hamptons on Long Island, they were, even in the '70s, a paradise for wealthy celebrities. During the summer we lived at the domestic abuse shelter, Southampton was also a haven for writers like Truman Capote, George Plimpton, and E. L. Doctorow. Like us, they arrived at the beach getaway with hearts full of hope and a desperate need for isolation. For them, the goal was to create. For us, our greatest wish was to live.

~ ~ ~

An uneasy wave of goodbyes escorted us from the safety of the shelter in early autumn 1977. Newcomers watched us prepare to leave. I wondered if they were thinking of the day when they would be free to live in the real world. The shelter staff got Mom a job at Maryhoken, a piece-work factory designed to give developmentally disabled individuals jobs. Mom was to be an aide. I found this ironic since we were hardly able ourselves.

A collective fear joined us as we drove away from the shelter. Enveloped in the shelter's support system, we were safe, cared for, and kept alive. Despite the desperation of its residents, the shelter had healed our helplessness. Close quarters and locked doors brewed months of belly laughs and the joy we had forsaken under Dad's roof.

I watched out the back window as we drove away, teary-eyed at the loss of my dear counselor. Lisa huddled with Joni and Rachel in front of room twelve. Joni raised her broken arm. A going away gift from her police officer husband, who'd broken it after she told him she was leaving. Her thick white cast wore a colorful collection of written assurances. Never again. You will heal.

Joni's daughter, Rachel, had not uttered a single word all summer. Joni shared the story of her husband's abuse at a Friday night powwow where residents chain-smoked cigarettes and nodded in solidarity. Her husband became my barometer of evil possibility, and our dark waters cleared a bit whenever I thought of it.

A zigzag of smolder rose from Joni's cigarette. "He was a real mother fucker," she said, taking a drag from the cigarette. The other women nodded. "Locked my six-year-old, Rachel, in the utility closet for three days. She's afraid of the dark, and I heard her sobbing the whole time. Snuck water in, and I tried to let her out. That's how I got this." She raised her cast. "All because Rachel spilled glue while making a paper-mâché dinosaur. That son-of-a-bitch."

"She took it hard. Won't talk no more. Ain't seen my baby smile in a year." Joni cried then, stomping the butt of the cigarette into the dirt and twisting until she'd buried it. As we drove from the shelter, Lisa held Rachel's hand in the air, trying to reanimate the young survivor. Rachel's little arm flopped as Lisa tried to wave her limp hand. She wore the stony mask of her abuse.

~ ~ ~

As the group disappeared, I turned to my brother who was looking at me for assurance. Laying my hand atop his, I reexamined the pristine mansions as we drove past. Mom slowed to avoid a long black limousine on the side of the road. We watched an attractive blond man—who we all thought was Robert Redford—exit the back. Movie stars were everywhere in Southampton, and spotting one gave me a rush of excitement and gloom. We had lived in the community for months but could not be farther from their reality.

The man looked angry as he kicked the flat tire that had impeded his journey. The driver exited next, bowing apologetically. Heated gestures followed.

"Too bad," Mom uttered.

"Yeah, too bad," I agreed.

The drive to the Patchogue apartment complex took forty minutes. A beehive of ugly brick buildings greeted us, each two stories with identical tar roofs and faded metal doors. Life in the shelter had prepared us for living in cramped, undistinguishable quarters. We unpacked our few belongings from the trunk in silence. We trudged across the asphalt parking lot, passing a group of Spanish-speaking teens, and they paused their handball game to let us pass.

We lugged our suitcases around building F twice before finding F-10. Peter set down his case as Mom fumbled with the key. Bars covered the street-level window. "We're moving into jail?" Peter asked.

"No. Those bars are to keep us safe," Mom answered.

"From who?" Peter looked confused.

"Bad guys." I ruffled my brother's hair as we entered the apartment.

"You mean Dad?" Peter asked seriously.

"Nope. Other bad guys. Don't worry. He can't get you anymore."
I was not convinced but hoped it was correct.

Inside, I felt along the wall, finding the switch to turn on the light.
A long living room and kitchen combo came into view.

"We have power, Mom." I had dreaded arriving at the apartment
to find it lacking electricity or furniture.

"Yep, the shelter paid the first two months. Look, we have a
couch too." Mom pointed to an overstuffed plaid three-seater, the only
furniture in the room.

Leaving our suitcases at the door, we hurried to explore the
bedrooms. "Yes," Peter jumped on one of two twin beds in the larger
bedroom. "I don't have to sleep with you anymore."

The second bedroom was bare except for a curtain rod and lever
shade. "Where's your bed, Mommy?" Peter asked.

"I guess they couldn't get one donated. I'll sleep on the couch for
now."

Mom settled on the worn sofa. "You kids must be hungry. Better
get the food from the car."

I volunteered. The teens we passed on the way in continued to
chase the pink handball as I walked back to the parking lot. The tallest
and darkest of them stopped to lean against the brick wall as I passed.
Grabbing the two paper sacks of food from the back seat, I locked the
car behind me.

Balancing the two bags, I passed the boy who was watching me.
His whistle startled me, and I walked faster. He laughed at my hurried
pace.

"Some boy whistled at me, Mom." I told Mom as soon as I
entered the apartment.

Mom smiled, "Well, you're a cute girl, and you're growing up."

A lot had changed in the months at the shelter. My girlish figure
had become curvier, but I never considered myself pretty. "You got

boobies." Peter chimed in from the kitchen, where he sat on the floor reading the comic book Lisa had given him before we left.

"Eww." I emptied the donated groceries into the empty cabinets. Looking down, I realized Peter was right. "We got bowls and silverware, Mom," I said, trying to divert everyone's attention away from my physique.

After eating a box of mac and cheese prepared with water for lack of milk, Peter raced around the apartment. Burning energy pent up for too many months in a tiny motel room, he giggled the entire time.

On his tenth lap, Mom demanded, "Enough, Peter. Settle down. I start my job tomorrow. Gotta get some sleep."

The apartment complex, with its petty thievery and poor reputation, was home for one year. Mom grew to love her job at Maryhoken and added a second retail position in a gift shop. Proprietor Flo Wentnick must have seen something good in Mom, for she hired her the moment they met at her gift shop, trusting Mom to close the shop that night. They have been friends ever since.

Food stamps and welfare kept us afloat as Dad fought child support and demanded weekend visitations. The first court-ordered visit came two months after the move.

"That man is not going to hurt you ever again. You have to see him for one day. He's taking you to the movies. It'll be fun." Mom did not sound convinced.

Peter moped all morning, returning to the silence that defined him before the shelter. I was outraged. "I don't understand why we have to see him. Doesn't the court know he beat you and Peter?"

"Yeah, they know," Mom answered. "He won't find out where we live," Mom looked at Peter. "We're meeting him at McDonalds. You can have apple pie."

Dad's truck was parked at the far end of the McDonald's lot, a beacon of danger. Mom pulled in next to him. He glared from the driver's seat, looking exactly as angry as before we left. Revulsion filled his eyes, his face not registering any appreciation for seeing his children after the long separation.

Undaunted and wanting to get the visit over, I took Peter's hand, pulling him towards our father. Dad opened the door, smiling like the Joker character in the Batman sitcom we watched daily at the shelter.

Peter moved behind me, cringing at the site of his abuser.

Dad nodded at Mom, who demanded, "I will meet you back here at five."

"Or what?" Dad asked. "You'll divorce me and steal my kids?"

"Just be here, Joe." Mom resisted the urge to scream. She wanted to remind him that visitation was torture for us and that he had stolen everything we owned, including the house we called home.

Mom watched from the car as Dad led us to the restaurant. We lagged far behind, looking back at her, desperate for relief. Mom cried as she drove from the restaurant to pass the five hours until Dad brought us back.

At the counter, we ordered quietly, not looking at Dad. The middle-aged woman at the counter asked, "What was that, honey? I can hardly hear you."

With Big Macs and fries in hand, we found an empty booth. Nibbling on the treats, we looked at our laps.

Dad cleared his throat in the full, throaty manner that predicted a proclamation or lie. I lifted my eyes a few inches, watching my father's hands. The hands that had previously appeared so large and calloused were different. A smooth moon of white shone at the end of each nail, covered in clear polish.

"You kids know dem people where you stayed were liars, right?" Dad's tone was disgusted. His voice boomed over the lunchtime crowd, and a mother dining close by gave him a dirty look.

His voice lowered to a snort. "Your mother's not a fucking victim. You were never hurt. Were you?"

In all its preposterousness, the question made Peter look at Dad as if he had horns protruding from his head.

"Yes, Dad, we were." I grabbed Peter's knee in a gesture of support.

"I never hit you." Dad pointed a manicured nail close to my face.

"No. But Mom and Peter..." I stopped the accusation mid-sentence, realizing we were stuck with Dad all day.

"What? What did I do to them that they did not deserve?" Dad's nose scrunched in disgust. He slammed down the burger, unleashing pickles and lettuce. "Everything's a fight with you. You're just like her."

I opened Peter's apple pie to let it cool, not looking directly at my father for the rest of the day. Fear of retribution was a more potent silencer than any gun could bear.

We ate in silence and followed the awkward lunch with a trip to the 112 Cineplex where we saw the movie *American Gigolo*. I had to cover Peter's eyes several times. The film was ripe with sexual content and inappropriate language.

In the lobby, bored and sickened by the day, I asked Dad, "Why'd you pick that movie?"

The answer defined the core of his personality, "Because I wanted to see it." In all his life, my father never once considered what was appropriate for anyone except himself.

Mom arrived at the parking lot early, watching families come and go. They laughed and hugged, enjoying the normalcy of life. She imagined them returning to three-bedroom homes with suites of comfortable furniture and closets full of non-donated clothing. Like most days, Mom wondered how many were hiding the same bruises she had concealed for seventeen years of marriage.

We pulled into the lot five minutes late. Mom approached the truck in a panic. "You're late." We sat mopey and miserable in the back seat. "Next time, get them here on time."

Dad puffed his lips, "I'm gonna turn the kid's rooms into monthly rentals. Interested?"

The barb struck its mark. The idea of strangers living in the rooms we ached for silenced Mom. Her face folded in defeat. Opening the back door, she hurried us from our father's clutches.

Silence saturated the car ride like a dangerous storm. Being forced to spend time with our abuser was too terrible for words. We recovered from the emotional crisis at home with heaps of mint chocolate chip cookies, a treat from the food pantry.

Peter inspected the fridge. Three eggs in a bowl, ¾ of a government cheese block, and a stick of margarine were all it held. "No milk, Mom?"

"No, they didn't have any in the pantry. We're out of food stamps until next month," Mom informed, crunching on a sweet but slightly stale cookie.

Every time we felt starved, I imagined my father in the Medford home, where he lived alone, at the full fridge, sliding half gallons of milk and juice to the side to reach a craved morsel. I saw his teeth bared, biting into something delicious. Each time we visited, his pantry was well-stocked, and the fridge overflowed. I pictured him munching and mumbling about my mother in the room where hundreds of family dinners once took place.

Divorce makes one hungry and jealous of the eaters.

26 Rocky Point

The winter of 1979 was exceptionally harsh on our little family as we moved into the third apartment after the divorce. Our first apartment, a two-bedroom unit at Patchogue Heights Apartment complex turned out to be a den of criminal activity.

Walking to and from the bus stop after school was a sordid affair. Drug dealers and drunks lined the sidewalk. "Come here, boy. Get over here. I wanna talk to you inside." The horrible man reeked of stale beer. I covered my nose, pulling Peter's book bag to make him walk faster. The man followed, reaching his cigarette-stained yellow fingers to try to catch us. His inebriated state slowed him to a sluggish pace. We got away.

"Mom, some gross guy tried to get us to go into his apartment today," I told Mom that night. The lease ended on Halloween. We moved the next day, again squeezing our belongings into the Maverick. Tony, a coworker from Maryhoken, transported the rest of our sparse, mismatched furniture in his pickup truck.

Our next home was a peeling apartment in a hundred-year-old house in Sayville. The house dripped with neglect and decay. We collected the rain that poured into our third-floor apartment in eight strategically placed buckets. Wood floors sagged, and heavy doors hung from hinges. A hunchbacked old man and his brother lived in one downstairs unit, and another divorced mom and her two kids in the other.

We stayed in the old behemoth for one year until the greedy landlord upped the rent, pricing us out of the place and forcing the move to Rocky Point on Long Island's North Shore.

Weeks of hard winter coated the concrete steps to the third-floor apartment in Rocky Point when we arrived. A senior citizen named Mary owned the place a block from the ocean and thirty-five minutes from our father.

Peter and I trudged up the front steps eighteen times that icy day, carrying boxes of belongings accumulated in the years post-shelter. Some also held treasured mementos from before, coerced from Dad during once-a-month visits.

Some boxes contained stolen goods, taken from the Medford house in a frantic rush while Dad was at work. Finding the locks changed, we broke in through the kitchen window, lifting Peter to squirm through the pulled-away screen. The gathering of our things felt like a victory, and we stuffed the Maverick until we could not see out the back or side windows.

The ugliness of divorce had taken a toll. Mom went to our Medford house that day still fearful she'd lose us to the monster's secure income and ample living space. To mark the triumphant reclaiming, she found the "Best Dad" statue I had begrudgingly given him on Father's Day, and with the same meat cleaver he'd held to her neck Thanksgiving Day, decapitated the statue.

We left the headless trinket in the sink along with shards from Dad's favorite beer stein which Mom smashed on the countertop with a strength I had wished for her in the dangerous times.

Court-approved visitations with Dad ended once Peter, no longer beaten, found his voice. "I'm not going," he announced one Saturday morning. The forcefulness of his words astonished me, and I quickly sided with my brother's brave proclamation.

A year after move-in, Rocky Point was home. We'd covered the slanted attic walls of our rooms with posters. Piles of laundry littered the floors, and stereo volume wars were commonplace.

Mom was at her day job at Maryhoken when the phone rang, interrupting our typical after-school routine of homework and snacking. I could hardly hear it over Pink Floyd's *The Wall* album, which roared at full volume.

"Turn that down," I yelled. "Gotta be another one of your girlfriends," I teased, grabbing the phone before Peter, who had grown tall, athletic, and popular, could run for it.

"Hello." Peter tried to take the receiver from my hand. I slid across the linoleum, stretching the long cord to reach my room, and slammed the door behind me.

Peter pounded on the sloppy paint of my sky-blue door, "Come on. Give it."

Dad's voice surprised me, sending a worrying bolt through my stomach. "I'd like to see you kids," he said. "There's a lot you got wrong."

I opened my bedroom door, holding my hand over the phone. "It's Dad." Peter frowned, raising a hand, and heading back to his room.

I held the phone away from my ear, sickened at the thought of spending another minute pretending that my father was worthy of visitation.

"I'd like to take you to Pat and Jim's." The well-played invitation started my mouth watering. It was my favorite restaurant from the days before. The owners adored my appetite for the baked stuffed lobster that was their specialty.

"Peter won't come," I informed him to see if I might garner a restaurant meal without subjecting Peter to my father's bull. During the last weeks of visitation, dinner with Dad included a menagerie of showy restaurants with menus we could barely interpret. At every outing, Dad spoke in an overblown tone that sounded sweet and snobby. To make things worse, he insisted on ordering the most expensive entrée on the menu, usually one that cost more than our weekly grocery budget. A dichotomy of delight at the treat of eating out and dismay over the slim pickings in our always-lacking pantry turned the dinners unbearable.

"That's okay. Just you and me," Dad answered.

I picked at the nail that held my *Chorus Line* Playbill. I wanted to believe my father had changed. I was always waiting for the dad from our childhood dance to emerge. I ached for a father to help prepare me for life, to put my needs before a showcase of travel souvenirs accumulated on trips to Germany, Turkey, and Italy.

"Yeah, Dad. I guess so," I agreed, craving good food but dreading the dissension into victim land.

"I'll pick you up at six," he said gruffly.

"He's just showing off for Pat and Jim. I don't see why you're going," Mom said. "You're just gonna get upset." Mom sat at the round wooden table, pulling off the sneakers she wore for her day job, which required eight hours of running back and forth between mentally challenged clients to guide them through assembly tasks.

"Sure, Mom, but lobster." I watched over Peter's shoulder as he struggled with spelling practice. Pointing to a mistake, I sounded out the word "Raaaaainbow." Peter erased his first attempt, rewriting the word correctly.

When the doorbell clanged its broken jingle, I kissed Mom. "I'll be back. Just dinner," I yelled, running down the worn carpet on the multi-colored steps.

By the time I got to the front yard, Dad was already back in his car. I opened the passenger door, nodding at Dad, who leaned in for a hug. I half-heartedly met his attempt at affection, shrugging at the hurt look on his clean-shaven face.

"Hey," was all I managed, watching the tree-lined street disappear, replaced by the familiar shops on Route 112.

We entered the restaurant to the usual hoopla of hugs from Jim, a gregarious Italian who loved his regular customers with enthusiasm. Jim gushed at Dad's pink dress shirt and smart slacks, turning his attention to me next and complimenting my usual high school attire of a blue denim skirt, vest, and black T-shirt.

"Welcome back, Ms. Vicki-lynn. I've missed you." Pat hugged me, and I hugged back.

Our regular spot was at the center of the gold and red dining room. It was a round table with chairs for four people and occupied by just that many on the days when we dined wearing plastic smiles that belied the violence.

Dad ordered a bottle of wine for himself and a Shirley Temple for me. Another habit from the *before* days. An appetizer of steamed clams had arrived before we had a chance to order. Dad showed off for the other diners with exaggerated thanks and kisses on our waitress Bonnie's cheek.

I watched Bonnie wipe the kiss away before she pushed open the swinging door that separated the dining room from the chef's domain. The gesture delighted me because it belied Dad's belief that the staff at Pat and Jim's Whirl Inn adored him.

We ate silently except when Dad handed me a pile of photos from his latest trip. All architectural and lacking humanity, they told the empty story of solo travel. Dad showed them off as if they were the culmination of a dream.

I looked at my father with the uniquely critical eye of a fifteen-year-old. His skin was clear and smooth.

I recalled a week when we'd eaten boxed mac and cheese five nights in a row and how Mom told us we would not get a support check because Dad was not working. My father had a keen ability to become conveniently unemployed right before child support court dates. The infrequency of his ironwork had begun to relieve Dad of his rough physical attributes.

The lobster arrived, pre-split down the middle, and filled with a buttered stuffing. I paused before digging into my favorite food. Hunger outranked the guilt I felt for enjoying the abundant meal. As soon as Dad filled his mouth with a slice of prime rib, I bowed my head, praying aloud. "Dear Lord, please let Mom and Peter have a good meal like this soon." Dad practically choked. I smirked into the first bite of savory goodness.

"Dad, we ate mac and cheese for a week this month," I remarked, trying to sound nonchalant.

"Well, your mother should budget better. I'm not a friggin bank." His voice grew stony. He seemed ready for the guilty onslaught I would deliver. It was a seesaw of banter that boiled up whenever we were together.

I continued eating, pausing mid-mouthful to remind him of my mother's employment status. "Mom works three jobs, Dad."

"Then she should have money for groceries." He put down his steak knife, which was unneeded due to the tenderness of the meat.

His throat-clearing grunts came at a rapid pace, a sign of agitation. "I don't want to talk about your mother. Can't we enjoy the meal?"

"Sure, but we need band and wrestling uniforms. It's not fair that you get the house and keep taking all these trips." I gestured toward the pile of photos.

His jaw tightened to reveal muscles and sinew, a sign of rising anger, "I save for those trips. Your mother has always been a spender. The woman can't manage money. Not my problem."

"But it's us too, Peter and I?" I finished my lobster, yanking the plastic bib from under my chin. Exasperated, I stewed at the depth of my father's insularity.

Dad looked around the restaurant, making sure no one was in earshot. Diners slurped spaghetti and soup, oblivious to the evil under his fancy façade. Dad leaned across to me, lowering his voice to a savage whisper, "I pay $30 a week for you and Peter. Your mother abandoned me with all the fucking bills and took you, kids. Someday you'll see how whacked she is. Now, I don't want to hear another Goddamned word about money or your fucking mother; you hear me?" His finger touched my nose, and I winced.

He settled back, the mask of pampered nonchalance returning. He was again a well-to-do guest treating his daughter to the priciest items on the menu.

Bonnie returned to see if we wanted dessert, "Banana split honey?" she grinned gently. Bonnie had seen my mother's bruises in the days when the family dined together, and she also witnessed how roughly Dad handled Peter after he spilled a glass of water. Bonnie saw through the façade and felt sorry for us.

"No thanks." I could not stomach dessert. I was busy stewing at my father's inability to acknowledge how his violent behavior caused the divorce or the multitude of ways he continued to fail us.

Dad ordered cheesecake, eating it slowly to remind me he owned my time.

Bonnie slid a small dish of ice cream to me, her eyebrows raised in a question. The metal bowl of vanilla goodness had a cherry at the center, surrounded by a delicate drizzle of hot fudge. I nodded an agreement that I would not allow my father's pomposity to ruin dessert.

Dad paid with a flashy gold credit card. Defending when he caught me eyeing it, "I pay it in full every month."

I bit the inside of my cheek to keep from speaking. I detested him. His dead eyes and arrogance gave me a queasy feeling in the pit of my stomach. Revulsion was the one storm I could not escape. At its center spun a whirlwind of want, grasping for signs of love in the nightmare that was my paternity. Like a whip against exposed flesh, spending time with Dad tamed the wild thoroughbred and survivor inside me.

We rode back to Rocky Point in silence. I slammed the door as I got out of his fancy car. Dad sped off, sending pebbles into the air with the rapidity of his acceleration.

Mom watched from the upstairs window, thankful I was home, and pained by the hurt and disappointment on my face.

27 High Times

The tarry sourness of the odor brings me back to Rocky Point every time I smell it. Like a cancer that kills the ability to move forward, the pot hung like a pungent cloud over the home where I completed high school.

Whether a means to relax from the three jobs she worked or a way to feel more akin to the young people that arrived with mine and Peter's social expansion, Mom's use of marijuana angered me for the ill-spent money and the way her smoking went against every anti-drug teaching she'd driven into my brain.

For me, marijuana smells like poverty. It always will.

~ ~ ~

I returned from college to the Rocky Point apartment where Mom and Peter still lived. Climbing the long flight of stairs with a knapsack on my back and a suitcase in hand, I instantly smelled my return to poverty. It was the familiar odor of money spent on munchies rather than utility bills. Dysfunction breeds dysfunction, and my mother continued the cycle of standing still by smoking marijuana joint after joint.

The smoking and drinking started long before I left for the state university. I tried it too but had such a severe reaction—putting my hand through the glass of my bedroom window—that I never smoked again.

I stepped into the apartment where Mom sat, the pipe in one hand and a cigarette burning in an ashtray. She watched me from a fuzzy space of stoned tranquility. "You're back?"

"Yeah, Mom, Joi dropped me off. It's Easter break, remember?" The ride from Buffalo to Long Island was a drawn-out, 500-mile journey that included a flat tire, an overheated engine, and the shared laughter of Long Island friends who had all chosen the university because it was the state college furthest from our parent's homes.

Peter sauntered down the hall to hug me hello. "Yo, Vic. Glad you're home," he said, before returning to the *Creature Feature* he and his friends were watching.

At fourteen, my dark Italian brother had grown lean and mature. With a quiet demeanor that most took for shyness, Peter attracted a crowd wherever he went. The fact that our mother allowed smoking and drinking in our home increased his attractiveness among teens in the township.

I left the group to party and went to my room. Opening the door, I found my bed piled high with the clean laundry that typically grew in my mother's room. Placing my suitcase next to the bed, I moved the pile of unfolded garments from my sleeping area. My hands were full of clothing when Mom opened my door, "I didn't forget you were coming," she yawned, stretching the tired muscles that were beginning to resurface as the pain-killing properties of the drug wore off. The daily grind of work and drug use dimmed Mom's stress and her ability to move forward.

I left for college directly after high school, intending to become an actress. My father refused to pay any portion of my college expenses, his meager child support payments vanishing as soon I turned eighteen. I excelled at acting in high school. However, the cutthroat competitiveness of the college theater program overwhelmed me. I was lost among the *normal* kids whose parents visited them on campus, handing out career suggestions, emotional support, and cash. Like my mother and brother, I struggled to find my footing. So, I drank too much at frat house parties, ditching morning classes and disregarding grade notices.

"Mom, you're stoned." Her lackadaisical attitude and the scene that welcomed me back to Rocky Point angered me. I wanted something normal. Meeting other students at college taught me that our third-floor life of drugs and partying was not it.

"Yeah, not much. I smoke when it's been a bad day. Calms things down."

"It's illegal." Mom stared at the wash pile, a million miles from our conversation.

"Come on. Let's get you something to eat." Mom changed the subject.

The pantry was better stocked than when I left. Food stamps and welfare were a thing of the past. Mom's raises at work and pilfering of soda bottles and cans brought into her job for deposit money had increased the economic outlook for the family from desperate to poor. When the bottles arrived at Maryhoken for recycling, someone had already claimed the nickel reward. Mom gathered the bottles in her trunk a few at a time and returned them in bulk for another go-round of deposit money. Desperation breeds ingenuity and thieves.

We settled on a bag of chips and onion dip from the fridge. I pulled the wooden captain's chair back, and my fingers became coated in thick dust. Dirt lined the windowsill and backsplash of the counter. Cleaning had fallen away as workdays melded into smoke, sleep, repeat.

"Mom, what are we doing for Easter?" I asked, licking the onion dip from a polished purple fingernail. My state college mates and I had painted our nails in the car, and my messy purple cuticles were a clear indication of the bumpiness of Interstate 86.

"Not sure. I hope Aunt Shelley and Uncle Ronnie will come over. Open house."

Thinking of the Silber family soothed my worry over Mom's smoking and the rotten state of the apartment. Ronnie Silber was the only person I'd ever seen calm my father's violent nature. Mom had phoned them dozens of times when we lived in Medford, and they always came. The Silber family was there whether we needed a ride to the emergency room, a shoulder to cry on, or a safe place to spend the night.

"Sounds good. I miss Aunt Shelley and Uncle Ronnie."

"They still see your father. There's something I have to tell you." Mom blurted the words in a slurred tone that was difficult to understand.

"What?" I crunched up the empty chip bag, sitting back as I stretched out my feet. My legs ached from twelve hours in the backseat of the Buick.

"Well, the last time they saw him, he was different."

I replied snidely, "He was born different, Mom. He's a monster."

"No. I mean, Dad was wearing, well, feminine clothes." Mom swirled her finger at the final gooey goodness of the onion dip container, licking it off her fingers in absolute disregard of how she looked with food on her chin and her tongue extended.

"What?" Road weariness dissipated like a rainbow. "He was what?"

"It was a pants suit, and Shelley said it was a women's outfit. He had his nails done too." Mom spilled the uneasy gossip as if discussing someone else's father. She wore the pleased look of a woman given clemency from years of guilt and abuse.

Her faraway look painted the information as casual and impersonal. Mom rose to throw away the evidence of our snack. Stepping on the peddle of the trashcan to lift the lid, she continued, "Well, he once dressed in my clothes for Halloween. Guess he liked it more than I thought."

"Mom, are you telling me that Dad wears women's clothes? Is he gay?" I swatted at the buzzing in my ears, annoyed that the front door was left open to allow in several mosquitos.

"No, he's still dating that woman. Or at least they are still traveling together. I heard they went to Spain last year." Mom wiped her dry mouth with the back of her hand, reaching for a water-filled Ronald McDonald glass.

"Then, what's with the clothes? Did you know about this? Did he wear your clothes?" I asked, astonished. The drugs coursing through Mom's veins made her loose-lipped and at ease with Dad's disorganized gender. I had no such chemical buffer, and the information put me in a dizzy state of disbelief.

Mom washed her hands, hovering over the pile of dirty dishes in the sink but not bothering to clean them. The sound of Peter and his friend's hysterical laughter arose and faded from the living room.

"Yeah," she continued, "that time we went to that psychologist together, they diagnosed him as a paranoid schizophrenic with homosexual tendencies. Guess they got that right." Mom laughed for a second but stopped when she noticed my stiff seriousness.

I stared at her in a dazed state of nuclear fallout. "Has he done this before, with Aunt Shelley, I mean?"

"Once, yes. I didn't think it was worth mentioning." Mom picked at her teeth with a toothpick retrieved from a small ceramic holder.

"Well, we'll talk after work tomorrow." The crooked owl clock on the peeling lemon wallpaper read ten past eleven. Mom's 6 a.m. alarm would sound too soon, and she'd regret it if she did not get to bed.

Astounded, I lay in my teenage bed. Incomplete images of my diabolical father in softly draped fabrics materialized and faded. Staring at four Broadway playbills stapled across my wall, I pictured the first thing that always came to mind when I thought of Dad: his clenched fists, hangnails, and rough skin. Plaid work sleeves and the full breadth of battle defined the man I called Dad. His masculinity gave me nightmares for the authority and pain of it. To cast him in soft attire that not even my tomboyish mother would don was unfathomable. So, I chose to forget, storing away the nugget of preposterousness for years.

28 Capitol Reunion

I grappled for years with the fragments of our father-daughter relationship, craving my father's attention but tremoring each time he resurfaced in my life. The thick, choking sound of his voice flung me back to defiance and the drawing of enemy lines. I wanted a father, but the past blinded me to any possibility that Dad might fulfill the paternal role. When I looked at Dad, I saw his hands hurling my brother into the wall and heard rainwater drip into the feline death cauldron.

Despite these nightmarish mental scars, I indulged in a minuscule hope of metamorphosis. Abandoning my father was not an option as long as I could recall the man who once held my hands as I balanced on his shoes to dance. So, when my brother Peter, in his second year of military service, decided to give our father a second chance, I followed suit.

~ ~ ~

Military life suited my brother. Following instructions spewed by Naval commanders was easy for him. He'd been bossed and bullied for a lifetime. Our father's sinful physicality toughened Peter. Basic training finished the job. The beaten boy grew into a good man whose physical strength and height dwarfed his childhood tormentor.

It was a lazy Sunday afternoon when Peter called, and I turned down the television once I heard his voice on the answering machine, rushing to pick it up. The protective panic learned in the Selbach household made me a prognosticator of bad news regarding Peter.

"Hey, punky, everything okay?"

"Yeah, yeah," he answered, brushing off the question. He had grown used to my worried inquiries. "Got an idea. Carol and I have a place right outside DC now. Why don't you come for a visit? See the sites."

"Doug can't get time off, and I don't drive. How would I get there, goofball?"

"Train?"

"No, uh, not happening. When I took Amtrak to see Mom in Davey, I could not sleep. I never heard so much snoring and so many baby cries in my life."

"Well, Dad could drive. He called me, and I let the machine get it as usual. But it sounds like it might be time to see him."

"Whoa. Is Dad dying? Never thought I'd hear you say that."

"Me either, been thinking. Like to see Daddy dearest try some of that shit now."

My heart lit at the suggestion of my brother's revenge and my father seeing how Peter had blossomed despite his best attempts at murder. "Yeah, I'd like to see you sock him just once."

"Whatever. I'm on leave in November. Maybe then?"

"Can't hurt to ask. Dad will give me crap about gas money."

"If he does, I'll pay it."

"Love you, Peter."

"You too."

~ ~ ~

195

Dad agreed to the visit.

I rode the bus from Boston to New York the day before the DC trip. Sporadic heat and the opening and closing doors at every stop chilled me to the bone. I had started the journey with a slight head cold that blossomed into an ugly geyser. By the time I arrived at the house in Medford, all I wanted was a nap.

Entering the painful remnants of my childhood home caught my breath. What was once a suffering chamber dwindled as I placed my case on the first step of the attic staircase. A green recliner sat in the corner near the door. I walked towards it, checking for the worn arms of my childhood. The fabric perfectly replicated Dad's first sulking throne. Uncomfortable revisiting the toxic hallway, I looked to where the cross had saved us twenty years prior. The tiny nail hole was gone, patched by a fresh coat of paint. I ran my finger over the raised stucco, looking for evidence of grace.

The hallway was shorter than I remembered. The killing closet seemed shrunken, too, much too narrow a space for my adult body. I peeked into my brother's room, almost expecting to see the red coverlet of his twin bed. I stared briefly at the corner where Peter had taken so many punishments. My eyes watered from a burgeoning head cold and the memory of his tiny body standing rigid in the spot for hours. I wiped my eyes, turning from the memory as Dad approached, "Why do you need two stoves?"

"I like to entertain," he defended, heading to the bathroom and closing the door before I could ask any more questions.

My pink room had a twin bed in the exact spot where my canopy once rested. The room was unmistakably mine despite a coat of eggshell paint and plaid curtains. I sat on the bed for a moment, remembering the prayers and pleading in that space. I wondered whether it was lunacy or hope that made me return to the place where I'd wished for Dad's demise.

A queen-size bed in my parent's room replaced the king my mother and father had shared. A pink floral quilt and crocheted pillow covers gave the room a feminine feel. Bled out, Dad's house felt blank and soulless.

Dad returned to the kitchen to check on the Sauerbraten and dumplings he'd prepared for my arrival. The heavy aroma of sour beef and dumplings broke through my congestion. It was a memory food he had served dozens of times in the years of cussing, hollering, and smashing.

In my parent's bathroom, I stood at the double sinks, recalling all the blood I'd wiped from the counter. I wondered if buildings held onto the physical energy of occupants. Can a house hate forever? I shuddered for whoever might live in the Medford house next.

I barely picked at the meat that Dad had taken hours to prepare. Anxious about our 5 a.m. departure and my thickening head cold, I set down my fork. "Dad, I'm not feeling great. Think I'm gonna hit the hay."

Lugging the small case to my room, I stopped in the hall to check the thermostat. "Hey, Dad," I yelled down the hall to my father who was washing the last pot, "can I turn up the heat? It's at sixty-two degrees. Freezing in here."

Dad barked back, "Sure, if you pay the bill. Leave it."

I shook my head, unwilling to engage the man I was about to spend six hours in the car with. Grabbing a handful of tissues, I went to bed.

Gazing at the ceiling, under which I had cried for many years, made me feel sicker.

Putting my hands together, I prayed, "Thank you, God for getting me out of this place and saving our lives. Amen."

197

I awoke to my father's voice, startled by a timbre I had not been awakened by in years. "Gotta go. Get up." Lifting my head off the bed, it felt heavy. In a flu-like fog, I dressed for the ride.

Head pounding and airways plugged, I sneezed three times over the bowl of cereal my father offered. Dad ignored my nasal voice and visible ailments. "All right, then. Wash that bowl, and we're headed out."

Ten minutes into the ride, I rested my head against the cold glass of the passenger side window, allowing myself to slip into much-needed slumber. Just as I fell into a deep sleep, Dad cleared his throat. "You gonna sleep the whole way? Some co-pilot."

"I'm sick, Dad. Just need some rest." I closed my eyes again, only to be reminded of my lapse of duty thirty minutes later. "Still sleeping there?"

"Yes, Dad." And so, it went for the six-hour drive to Washington. I dozed on and off while he chastised me for neglecting my duty to keep him entertained as he drove.

We called Peter from a pay phone in DC, deciding to meet near the Lincoln Memorial. I hugged my brother warmly as soon as I spotted him. Dad and Peter shook hands.

"This is my girlfriend, Carol." Peter introduced the attractive blonde who nervously fidgeted next to him. I hugged her, too.

We toured the US Capitol, taking pictures of the snow-covered White House lawn and the heartbreaking expanse of the Vietnam Wall.

Peter and Dad did not address each other directly. Instead, we women kept the conversation going. "Can you believe all the names?"

"So sad," Carol marveled. A somber mood surrounded the 246-foot structure. People spoke in the same hushed tones usually reserved for churches and libraries.

Dad looked at his map. The solemnity of the memorial seemed lost on him. "We better get something to eat."

Escaping the cold, we ate burgers at a local pub that Dad found in the *Zagat's* book he'd ordered for the trip. "They have twenty-eight different brews of German lager," he announced, leading us to the restaurant.

Dad monopolized lunchtime conversation, talking about his recent vacation to Germany. "My relatives drink bigger steins of beer than this awl the time, and some of dem are in their nineties. You shoulda seen the room I stayed in. Best in the city. Don't mind spending a few bucks on myself as long as it's clean."

Peter listened to our father's endless travel soliloquy, leaning to his girlfriend's hair to whisper, "He's still an asshole. Never asks anyone about themselves. Always about him."

I overheard him, hiding my smirk with the tissue I was using to wipe my nose.

Peter and I exchanged a knowing glance as Dad continued, "Did I tell you? I ordered the most amazing oriental rug in Turkey. It took two months to come, and I thought they ripped me off. But it made it. I put it in the dining room. It looks great with the Mahogany dining room set. That set has to be worth a few thousand bucks." He barely took a breath, delivering a checklist of values for each piece of furniture.

Peter crossed his eyes, and Carol almost spit out the soda she was drinking.

We visited with my brother, who had to be back on duty at Andrews Air Force the next day, for five hours. On the long walk back to the car, Peter and I walked ahead of Carol and Dad. Carol was telling him about the great tips she earned at her waitressing job, unaware that our father thought waiting tables and other manual labor was beneath him.

"Sorry. He's such a shmuck. Felt like we weren't even there at lunch."

"Yeah. No worries, sis. Some things never change. Some ego for such an asshole."

"You know he wouldn't let me sleep in the car. Even with this cold."

"You expected more? This is the same guy who made me sleep in the snow because I didn't do my friggin' homework."

"I forgot about that. I asked Dad to turn up the heat last night, and you would have thought I asked for his kidney."

"You vil freeze and you vil like it," Peter teased in an awkward German accent. "Seriously, how's the house?"

"Your room is his second kitchen."

"No shit? I coulda used that on the nights when Dad sent me to bed without dinner."

"Yeah," memories of the man who walked behind us flooded in, and my brother changed the subject.

"How's Mom?" Peter asked.

"Okay, I guess. She sounds tired. She and Lenny never go outside. They've joined the shade zombies in Florida."

"Yeah, well, I gotta get going. Rush hour here is worse than the Long Island Expressway."

"Longest parking lot in the world," we said in unison and laughed.

I stopped to hug Peter, a gesture always fraught with emotion. "Love ya, punky."

Peter leaned into the protectiveness of the hug, a reassurance. It was the hug of a thousand bruises, a hundred hospital visits, and dozens of near-death experiences. "Love you too, weirdo."

Dad was in a hurry, making goodbyes easy. My brother and father exchanged awkward nods. I hugged Carol and watched them cross the frozen lawn toward the Capitol building. The rush of pride that came next made it easy to ignore his comment.

"You gonna stand there all day? We gotta get the car and head to Monticello. I told you we were gonna see it today."

PART III – MY TURN

29 Parental Introductions

Two and a half decades after my adoptive parents paced the sidewalk outside the Children's Relief Building, hoping to spot the woman who gave them a daughter, it was Dad's turn to meet my first mother.

My mothers had met a year prior, on an evening that felt like it would send Earth flailing into the Sun. Mom shared the milestones of my childhood with my biological mother, Anne. Jealous and naturally threatened by my first mother, Mom relished the ownership exposed by the retelling. Anne gulped Chardonnay and balled her eyes out for all she had missed.

After that blitzkrieg, I hoped I was through introducing my parents to each other. But Joe would not back down, asking about Anne every time we spoke. So, a year after Anne and Lillian met, my father waited at my biological mother's door, dripping sweat from the top of his bulbous nose and wearing a sour expression that exposed his lifelong aversion to humidity.

~ ~ ~

The year was 1994. I sat in my first mother's dining room surrounded by found family. The colorful menagerie of my bloodline included my half-sister and her husband visiting from Canada, my half-brother who still lived with Anne, and Doug, whom I had met at Fredonia State and married in Rockport, Massachusetts in 1991 after seven years of cohabitation.

A sense of casual acquaintance joined us at the table as the novelty of finding them faded. I felt comfortable with the family I looked so much like and secretly dreaded my adoptive father's arrival. *What will they think of the monster?* I wondered, tapping my fingers on the chair until Doug took my hand to settle my nerves.

The doorbell sounded, startling me, and I spotted Dad through the glass panel of Anne's front door. He had planned the trip without my consent, announcing his plans after I called to say we wouldn't be able to spend Easter with him. He'd invited us three times.

"Why not?" he'd asked, sounding annoyed.

"Going to see my birth mom. She invited us for spring break. My sister will be there. In from Canada."

"Well, then I'll come down. I'll take yew to Disney. The whole crew."

"No, Dad, it's sweltering this time of year. You won't like it." I replied, desperate to keep him away.

"I'll be fine; book a flight after we hang up." The line went dead. Dad had decided.

"Someone going to let him in?" Anne chimed, placing the last dish in the dishwasher.

Doug and I looked at each other like couples do when danger is imminent. He squeezed my hand as my sister opened the door.

"Hi, I'm Lidia; Vicki-lynn's over there." She pointed.

My father's hair was bright blond and teased into a coif that fell to his shoulders. His bare arms were hairless, as was his face. He stared at me, and I began to perspire.

Anne joined us in the vestibule while wiping her hand on a dish towel.

"Dad, this is Anne," I said, remaining seated.

Anne gave my father a long look, examining his spit-shined shoes, creased tan slacks, and a pierced ear. "Hi, it's nice to finally meet you."

Dad cleared his throat. "I brought you dis," he said, handing over a gold-wrapped bottle.

"Thank you," Anne raised an eyebrow as she unwrapped the gift. It was a pricey Cabernet she had seen executives order at bank celebrations.

The room grew silent until my sister's husband announced, "I'se hungry as a moose."

Dad checked his watch. "Well, our reservation is in an hour. I hope you don't mind," he looked at Anne. "I reserved the best table at the *Chart House*."

"Wow. Well, sure. If that's what you want. I mean, that's a pricey place for a group this size."

I scratched my sunburned arm nervously as Dad approached for a hug. I flinched when his hand came back, a reflex learned in the days when he doled out physical damage by the fistful.

"Hi, Dad." He smiled, looking at the French manicured acrylic nails I'd had applied for vacation.

"Very nice," he held my hand, admiring my nails until Anne interrupted.

"Come into the living room; make yourself comfortable," she called.

Anne offered him iced tea. He accepted, seemingly unfettered by meeting the woman who bore me.

Anne looked disappointed. Sitting on the teal leather couch with the recliner extended, she questioned him. "I hear you were an ironworker. Sounds like interesting work?"

"Yeah, the union gave me a hefty pension. Not hurting for nuttin' 'cause of it."

205

Always about the money, I thought.

Aware of the poverty that plagued Peter, Mom, and me in the post-divorce years, Anne narrowed her eyes. "Aren't you still in the same house where Vicki-lynn grew up?"

"Yeah. Lillian couldn't afford shit, so I got it. Wouldn't recognize the place now. Added an extra kitchen so I can entertain."

"Oh, she replied, "You entertain a lot?"

"Not as much as I'd like. But more than with the kids around, a real handful. Don't miss them years."

"Uh-huh." Anne nodded, "If you'll excuse me, I have to get ready for dinner."

She lowered the recliner and poured herself a glass of Chardonnay before escaping to her bedroom.

I followed. "You okay? I know he's, uh, different."

Her eyes filled as she gulped the wine. "That man has no idea what I would have done to be able to raise you. I can't believe he called you and Peter a handful. He was lucky to have you."

"I know." I sat on the bed next to Anne, thinking of the details not yet revealed. The severity of the abuse and his habit of wearing feminine clothing seemed too harsh a truth to bestow on my biological mother so soon after the reunion.

"He's not the father I pictured for you. I'm sorry, and I better get ready."

"Me too," I answered, heading to the guest room to do the same.

~ ~ ~

The Daytona Beach Chart House sparkled alongside the yacht-lined marina. As our noisy group of eight approached, a speedboat revved past, appearing to dance on the smooth water of the Intracoastal Waterway.

Inside the lobby, I chewed the inside of my cheek as Dad approached the maître d'. "Selbach. Joe Selbach."

"Yes, sir, we have a table for eight downstairs."

"Downstairs? I specifically requested a view."

"Here we go," I whispered in Doug's ear.

"Sir, I assure you the downstairs is lovely."

"Look, I'm paying for the best. So dat's what I want. That one looks good." He pointed towards a large table close to the window.

"Well, let me see what I can…"

Dad leaned into the man so close that I was sure the maître d' could smell the Listerine on his breath. "I'm here for an exceptional birthday, and I'll take dat one."

Anne squirmed, stepping from side to side. "It's beautiful. I don't care where we sit. Just being here is a treat."

Dad would have none of it. "He's gonna get that one ready. You deserve the best."

Dad waved over a passing waiter, who leaned close to hear my father whisper. I could tell by the look on the twenty-something's stoic expression that Dad was already making enemies.

Dad led us to the table of his choice, pulling the end chair out for Anne. "No, Joe. You should sit there."

Dad replied, "The birthday is yours, and so is the head spot." He sat to her left, and I quickly squeezed past the group to sit on her right for easy damage control.

Another waiter approached, and I smiled at him sheepishly, hoping my father would go easy. "To start," he announced loudly enough to silence everyone, "I want a bottle of your most expensive champagne."

"Dad?" I wanted to crawl under the table.

"No, thank you. That's far too extravagant," Anne asserted.

"For my daughter's real mother, nothing is too expensive."

The knowledgeable waiter bowed, wearing a look that made me know he'd experienced showy diners before.

I thought of the handiness of the description. My real mother to Dad was the woman who bore me, not the woman who fell to the floor under his abuse or worked three jobs to be sure I had a marching band uniform and three meals a day. He needed to worship Anne to show me that some people deserved lavishing while others did not.

The family spent the entire meal squabbling and complaining about the entrees' diminutive sizes and costs.

"I needs another beer," demanded my sister's husband, Bob, in a thick Canadian accent I had trouble deciphering. The waiter arrived with salads, and eager for the distraction, I dug in, filling my fork with the tangy sweet leaves of a Caesar salad.

Bob ate his salad in a great rush, watching everyone else finish and fidgeting in his seat. Bob stood as I placed my fork across the etched glass bowl, holding a hand to his heart. "Sometins wrong."

My half-sister followed her husband, touching his back, looking back longingly at the rolls delivered as they walked to the lobby. "Jesus, Lidia, if I knew what the fuck it was, I would be a doctor now, wouldn't I?" Bob shouted, and at least three groups of patrons looked up.

Dad's brow moistened.

Lidia took her distraught husband from the restaurant.

My half-brother Jim reached for the rolls. "I ain't waiting on them." Slathering a butter ball across the top of the baked goods, he ingested the roll in two bites.

Anne's husband, a retired garbage man from Staten Island, spoke next, "Someone should check on dem. He looked sick."

"He's a drama queen," Jim argued. "Lidia's with him. He's okay."

"Excuse me for worrying," Senior sputtered, annoyed by his son's tone.

"How about worrying about him ruining my meal with his bullshit."

Two wait staff arrived carrying heavy trays filled with our meals. Jim Senior stood, nearly knocking over the waitress behind him. "Well, Buddy. I'm gonna check on your sister."

"Suit yourself," Jim chimed, lifting the hamburger to his waiting mouth. With a mouth full of food, he said, "Poor Lidia, Poor Bob. Such bull."

Senior turned back, shouting, "At least she's got a job."

"What are you saying, Dad, I'm lazy? I'm eating here. Go look after your baby girl."

Jim put his burger down, storming past his father to leave. Senior followed. Leaving Doug, Anne, Dad, and I alone to stare at the dumbstruck waiters, who, unsure whether to deliver meals to the empty settings or recover them, looked at Dad for an answer.

"Just leave them. It's der problem if the meals are cold."

I eyed the lobster I'd ordered, recalling the childhood melees whenever my father's meal was interrupted. A slight reddening of his cheeks revealed the seething behind his calm tone.

Doug and I looked at each other, eating as Dad poured Anne a second glass of the pricey champagne. My first mother looked exasperated, her eyes darting from the table to the door for signs of the rest of her family.

"How's your fish?" I asked, trying to lighten her mood.

Dad answered, "Fresh caught. Has to be good."

Anne nodded, looking back at the door.

Ten minutes later, Bob and Lidia returned smiling and acting as if nothing occurred. "Forgets I caint eat romaine. Gets me here," he pounded his chest. "One good belch, and I'se good as new." They returned to their seats.

A few minutes later, my half-brother returned, the thick smell of cigarette smoke trailing with him. "Dad's coming. He's tawkin to a couple from Queens, here for the races."

Dad cleared his throat, "Good. Eat up. That dinner cost more than a race ticket."

Anne choked at the comment. Her eyes narrowed as she changed the subject, "Have you been to the speedway?"

"No. Too hot on them bleacher seats. I'll take a good bottle and a view over that crap anytime."

Anne nodded. I interjected, "Dad's not outdoorsy. The only time he went out as a kid was to mow the lawn," *and drown cats,* I thought.

Jim Sr. returned next, talking fast, "Nice folks I met out dere. Cupla New Yorkers. Told dem about Booth's Bowery and a couple of other places to eat that ain't a rip off like dis place."

His forehead as red as the lobster tail, my father answered, "Zagats gave this place five stars. Do you know what it takes to get dat gooda rating?"

Senior sliced his steak, raising his knife to say, "A steak's a steak. Aint gotta pay thirty bucks for dis, not while Booth's has a $10.99 special on Fridays."

Bob and Lidia nodded in agreement, and I watched my father squirm at the unappreciative comment.

"I hope you're enjoying your meal, Anne." He focused on her.

Looking embarrassed, overwhelmed, and relieved that Dad did not reach across to squash her five-foot-three husband, she said, "Yes. I think I'm ready for a refill; she downed the last of the champagne in her glass.

My father poured her another glass, then lacing his fingers atop the table, he stated, "I hope you left room for dessert. I ordered something big time."

The family continued to talk and chew, ignoring my father's comment. I grinned as he bit the inside of his cheek. "Cheers, Anne," I said, raising my glass in her direction.

"Cheers," she answered, shaking her head.

"The circus is coming to Orlando," my half-brother interjected into the rumble of conversation among the now merry group.

Well, it's already been to Daytona, I thought, smiling.

30 Baby Mine

From the moment that I found out I was pregnant, the idea of allowing Dad near my child sent me into a panic. I wanted my baby to know the father I imagined, not the Daddy I feared. I worried he'd snap back into the years when his wild, unpredictable temper reigned supreme, and narcissism was the easiest of his personality disorders to manage. The mellowing effects of age and Dad's constant guise of social importance and goodness did not ease my cautious tendency.

When I was a child, Dad perceived himself above others, alienating them with raging fists, swift kicks, bigotry, and racism. As a more experienced man, he dialed down his anger to mask his sordid upbringing and the families he'd abandoned. Being around him made me uneasy. Prey cannot trust the hunter after peering down the barrel of his gun.

Access to my child would be limited. Still, I needed Dad to know her. Perhaps a second chance would give me recompense for his transgressions. I hoped the interest Dad showed in his grandchild meant he was ready to rise above his petty ego and impossible expectations.

~ ~ ~

"It's Dad. I'm in Boston. Please have Doug call us as soon as you go to the hospital. Bye." The machine burped the message as the cassette ribbon twisted. I sat in the living room of our two-bedroom apartment, rocking through a contraction. The miracle of birth started at 7 a.m. with a squeeze that made me laugh. Five hours later, under doctor's orders to stay home until contractions were minutes apart, nothing was funny. Thirty-two hours after the first twinge, I held my daughter.

The phone rang once. Dad's travel partner and companion, Millie, answered. "Hello. Yes, he's right here." She covered the mouthpiece. It's Doug."

Nervous, he cleared his throat, taking the phone, "Hello."

"Hey, Joe. Doug here. Your granddaughter has arrived. Thirty-two hours of labor, so she's too tired to talk. But everyone's okay."

"Wonderful. Thank God it's a girl. I'll be there tomorrow." He hung up before my husband could protest.

North Shore Hospital is fifty minutes from Millie's brownstone in Boston's Back Bay. As was his habit, Dad arrived early. The ring of the bedside phone woke me. Nia lay in my arms, sleeping. Doug grabbed the receiver quickly, hoping to avoid waking the baby. "It's your father. He's in the lobby."

My stomach lurched, and I held Nia—pronounced Naya—a bit closer. "Okay. Let him come up."

Through the rectangular window in the closed door, I spotted him. His cane, a prop he used to assure that no one doubted the permanently disabling knee injury he'd inflicted on himself with several crushing blows from a hammer, hung from his arm.

Nia woke, screaming hungrily. Breastfeeding was one clumsy misstep after another, and I worried that the child might starve.

Dad tapped on the door lightly. ·

"Come in." Doug was on his feet, opening the door.

213

"Oh, Dad. You made it," I said, the hard-edged tone usually reserved for our visits gone due to exhaustion.

Doug rejoined his friend, Brian, who lived close by, and arrived as we moved from the birthing room to a private room. The friends ate chips and joked.

"I'm the grandfather." Dad extended his hand to Brian, who wiped his salty palm with a napkin before responding, "Doug and I are old friends."

Dad looked at me next. Oblivious with exhaustion, I struggled to breastfeed Nia under a blanket draped across one shoulder. "Doug, can you call the nurse? I can't do this."

Brian stood, "I'll be outside."

Covering my breast, I pulled the cotton blanket back, revealing the baby to her grandfather for the first time.

He approached the bed with a rare timidity.

"This is Nia, Dad."

He shuddered, and I wondered if he understood the sanctity of someone so pristine, without sin or experience. Placing the flowers next to a cup of ice, he looked at my dark-haired child.

"They say that black hair will fall out. Ruffling the baby's hair, I continued, "You can already see the blonde underneath."

"Can I hold her?" he asked.

I grew breathless, staring at my father a full minute before answering, "Yes, but be careful."

He reached for Nia, and I held her for an extra second before releasing her swaddled body. She appeared tiny and vulnerable in his great arms, the same arms that swung so wildly with harmful intentions. Nia fussed a bit before settling in. I watched her breath rise and fall, enamored and taken with my child.

"Can I have her back? You'll drop her," I panicked.

214

Dad inspected his granddaughter's mane of dark hair and the plump cheeks, swollen still from the process of escape. "I ain't gonna drop her. Give me some friggin credit."

I fidgeted under the covers, feeling I might leap up at any second to retrieve my baby. Doug intervened, removing the soft comfort from my father's arms. He stood alone at the center of the sterile room, unsure of what to do next. Doug placed Nia back in my arms, and my shoulders relaxed.

Dad cleared his throat. I looked up, catching the anger in his eyes. He crossed his arms, "When you go home?"

"Tomorrow," I answered, quickly adding, "but no visitors. We want to be alone for a while. We need to get used to being parents, and we want to get it right."

Unaffected by the dig, Dad announced his intentions like a drill sergeant. "Well, I'm gonna bring Millie. A short visit ain't gonna kill yew."

"I said no visitors," I challenged, looking at Doug for a backup. "I'm exhausted, Dad."

"Well, I'm gonna take some pictures before I go."

I held my newborn close to my cheek as he snapped a dozen photographs. Nia began to cry as I lowered her to my shoulder. Agitated, I snapped, "Okay, that's enough."

He insisted, "Just a couple more."

"I said no, Dad. I make the rules here. It's not like with Mom and Peter; you're not in charge anymore."

The comment swapped the soft, pink hue of the room with bright, white hate, "What's that supposed to mean?"

"Nothing. I think you better go. I'm tired. Drained."

Dad removed the lens from his camera, wrapping it in the black cushioned cocoon of the case. He packed the camera's body next, tucking a cleaning cloth over the top. Satisfied that his thousand-dollar

215

investment was secure, Dad walked toward the bed. I held up my hand, a stop sign he heeded.

"Fine," he said. "Call as soon as you're up to visitors."

"Mm, hmm." I closed my eyes to block his hurt look. I had reason to mistrust him, but that did not flatten the bottomless embankment of emotions swirling in my head.

"Alright, I'll call in a couple of days." I opened my eyes as Doug extended his hand to shake Dad's. He shrugged the camera strap onto his shoulder, taking Doug's hand limply. That's when I noticed his nails. Each tip was a bleached white crescent, perfectly smooth and a tad longer than my own. He lingered, hand in hand with my husband for a moment too long, and Doug pulled away, moving to sit on the bed with us.

My heart raced, and Doug kissed my cheek, wearing a consolatory smile.

Dad turned to leave, mumbling, "You'd think I was gonna kill it or something."

31 First

A tangle of pink paper streamers greeted Dad at Nia's first birthday party, twirling from the small white fence that separated our lawn from the rocky ledge. He was late. A paper plate loosed as he approached, flying like a Frisbee to the middle of the mile-wide saltwater inlet. Doug and I rented a one-bedroom apartment in the Essex River home, where low tide bubbled with hidden mussel beds and creatures that, once freed by the incoming tide, would brush against swimmer's thighs, frightening them in the dark water.

Walking towards us, Dad stopped to point at something near the floating dock we shared with the ninety-year-old owner of the house. Called Nana Gumdrop by her grandchildren for the candy she hid around her camp-style kitchen to bestow upon them every time they visited, to us, she was Florence, a devout woman who watched Mass daily at a volume that assured we, too would be proselytized.

Dad's bleached hair was longer than I remembered and styled in soft under-curls. But it was the large, pink polka dot package that gave his entrance the head-turning effect he craved.

"Where you want this?" Dad shouted across the tiny backyard, where young men in short sleeve polos and women in flirty sundresses sat scattered in aluminum chairs. It was a typically adult first birthday crowd, consisting primarily of coworkers from my job at a semiconductor company.

I stepped from the back portico, "Right here, Dad. I was getting ice." Lifting the bag of quickly melting cubes, I hurried to dump its contents into the cooler full of bottled Coronas and colas.

Millie came up behind me as I finished, hugging me as I arose from the stooped pour. "Where's the birthday girl?" she asked, handing me two envelopes.

"Inside with Doug. He's changing her diaper."

"Where should I put this?" Dad held the gift high, ensuring everyone noticed the professional creases and fabric bow of the gift wrap.

I looked past Millie, "Over there with the rest of the gifts, Dad."

Once relieved of the gift, Dad stood among the sitting guests, rubbing his hands together as he assessed the princess-themed decorations. A jet ski buzzed past on the inlet, creating a slight wake. Conversation ceased until the rumble of the soulless machine dissipated.

"Joe. Joe Selbach." I heard Dad introduce himself, his feet sinking into the lush lawn. His presence created a moment of shaded relief over each guest as he towered over them. "I'm the grandfather," he bragged, until Millie tapped his shoulder.

"Here she is," Millie said, and everyone looked up, mesmerized by the white summer dress and glistening blonde hair of the baby Doug carried. Nia squinted as we put her in her highchair, curious and cautious at the applause. The chair decorated with balloons and streamers looked more like a throne than a mealtime perch. She sat at the center of the open porch, surrounded by dozens of wrapped presents.

From the center of the small lawn, he clasped his hands and asked, "Where did you find a crown to match dem shoes?" Nia pulled the rhinestone tiara from her head as if on cue, dropping it to a shady spot beneath the white parasol clipped to the back of her highchair.

Nia scrunched her nose in disapproval at the plate of sliced hot dogs Doug delivered. Millie asked if she could help, and I handed her the *Winnie the Pooh* plate. Millie fed her patiently, alternating tiny pieces of meat with slurps of grape juice from the matching *Tigger* cup.

"So, what'd you get her?" Dad blurted to a tall redheaded guest, "It ain't gonna be nothing compared to my gift. I'll tell you right now. It cost a fortune." The young woman covered her mouth with a *Pooh* napkin, nearly choking at the question.

"Um, a Doctor Seuss book. *Horton Hears a Who*," she answered.

"Yeah. Well. I ain't gonna ruin the surprise, but this grandpa got a whole hell of a lot more than that."

The ginger slipped away to share Dad's rude comment with our coworkers. The women glared at Dad, until the arrival of the half-sheet cake broke their horrified stare.

The ice cream cake began to melt in the July heat. White and pink piped icing creamed where it met the plastic platter. I started the song quickly, "Happy Birthday, dear Nia...."

Nia's fingers found the gooey cold icing and tapped at the cake tentatively. Dad, probably recalling my first cake-crushing fun, urged her on. As the last note of the traditional song faded, Dad boomed, "Dat's right, just like your mother. Mess it up good little piggy." He walked up to Nia and, taking both her hands in his, lowered them into the melting quicksand, oblivious to the wax number one candle burning at the center of the cake.

I reached for his hand. "Stop, Dad." It was too late. Before I could stop him, he had lifted Nia's chocolate-dripping hands to her mouth, purposefully smearing her cheeks with a sticky mess. As he rubbed, the candle toppled, rolling from the tray to the lawn, where it singed a cocktail napkin.

Nia, who did not understand what had happened, burst into tears at the sticky cold mess. The sugary concoction melted down her neck, staining the embroidery of her special birthday dress. She wiped her hands on the only thing handy, her hair, and the awkward, bawling scene exploded.

"What are you doing, Dad? We wanted to get pictures. For God's sake." Stamping on the napkin and crushing the candle in two, I screamed over the child's howling, "You ruin everything. Everything. Who said you could touch her? You don't get to touch her. Do you hear me? You don't get to touch my daughter. Look what you did to her cake and her dress."

Millie, a calm captain in every storm my father stirred up, handed the soupy cake to Doug. "Please put it back in the freezer. I'll get her cleaned up."

Doug downed his Corona in one long pull and obeyed, carrying the cake in front of him to keep it from dripping on his bare feet.

Millie unlatched the highchair tray, swatting at a yellow jacket drawn to the sweet aroma of my now sugar-coated child. Nia continued to wail, reaching for Millie, who tried to lift her from the waist, the one place not covered in ice cream. Carrying the baby, Millie glared at Dad. I followed her into the house.

As the door slammed, I heard Dad say, "Geez, we been here two hours. I hope they open my gift soon."

Doug returned with a fistful of beers, shaking his head. "We'll try that again after they get her cleaned up." He increased the volume to lighten the mood. Lyrics from a Will Smith movie filled the air, referencing damsels in distress and the losing of dresses.

Doug raised his beer, "I'll drink to that." The group snickered, returning to the conversation and drinks they had enjoyed before the cake scene erupted.

Dad brought the highchair tray to the hose, rinsing it off before replacing it. He wiped the chair next, using the last of the *Pooh* napkins.

220

Tossing the mess into the trash, he turned to the presents next, arranging them so his was at the front.

The screen door slammed, and everyone watched Millie emerge with Nia, who was clean and wearing her favorite mermaid dress. Behind her, I carried the somewhat lopsided cake back to the highchair.

Dad moved towards us. I raised a warning finger, lighting a birthday candle found in the junk drawer. While Doug took pictures, I restarted the birthday song. The group sang along. I leaned over Nia to help her blow out the crusty candle, then quickly sliced mounds of cake into waiting paper bowls.

Presents came next. I moved Dad's gift to the side, opening packages from Mom first. A jack-in-the-box, three sets of clothes, and a unique first birthday picture frame. Dad frowned, "That's all she sent her frigging granddaughter for her first birthday."

Millie defended, "Joe, you know she had to ship it from Florida. Gets expensive."

"Yeah, well, she should budget better. Pathetic."

I helped Nia open every single present except Dad's. He fidgeted every time I nudged the large package over, fraying the edge of the perfect paper. When there were no more options, I took Nia from the highchair to reach the enormous box.

Nia stood, swaying a moment on her toddler's legs. I sat next to her, helping her tear the paper. Tackling the cardboard box next, I pulled the wooden horse from the box, scattering foam popcorn pieces across the porch.

Dad brimmed with pride over the wooden rocking horse with its real horsehair mane and floral-etched leather saddle, snapping photos as fast as he could. He kneeled to get just the right angle. Nia looked at the horse, patted its mane, and turned to pick up the jack-in-the-box. "Mama Do," she said, and I wound the mechanism on its side until the clown jumped from its hiding place.

"Boo," I said. Nia giggled, "Again. Again."

Dad interrupted, "Put her on the horse. I want a picture."

"She wants to play with this first. One second, Dad."

"Well, we got company coming over. We gotta get going."

I raised my eyebrows, nodding. "Alright. Come on, Nia. You want to ride the horsey?" Placing her on the saddle and handing her the reins, I rocked the horse slowly.

Nia panicked, reaching for me. "All done," she said.

"Leave her there a minute," Dad jostled for another picture. Adjusting the lens, he moved closer.

"No, no." Nia lifted her arms high, indicating that I should remove her from the horse.

"One more," Dad ordered, fumbling for the perfect frame, light, and shade.

Nia began to cry. Dad kept taking pictures. "That's good. Gotta captcha the bad stuff too. Keep her there. Heh."

I got between him and Nia, bending over to obscure his view. "Dad, she's miserable."

"She'll survive. I'm almost through. Dad nudged my leg to get me out of his way, and I pushed back. "No, you are done now. Thank you for the gift. I'm sure she'll play with it later."

Millie grabbed his arm. "Come on, Joe; we have to get back anyway."

"That horse set me back two bills. I gotta at least get a decent picture."

"She's one, Dad. She doesn't care what it cost you."

Dejected, Dad frowned. "Well, you betta teach her. Like I taught you kids."

"What did you teach us?" I whispered, thinking of all the beatings and how much I wanted to punch him.

"Thank you for inviting us," Millie interjected as my defenses churned into gear.

Distracted by the radio Doug had turned up even further, Dad grumbled a few half-hearted goodbyes. I saw Dad one more time after the party.

31 Final Sight

Dad, are you transgender?

What would the day have brought had I asked the question? If I had known it was the last time I would see Dad, I might have hugged the man goodbye. I might have pardoned his impossible gruff behavior that night and kissed his rough cheek, recalling the goodness he expressed when I was the only Selbach child.

Or, it might have gone exactly as it did, for I was not ready to untangle the truth of Dad's gender. I was still aching for my Daddy. I wanted to be the top dog, the little girl wrapped around his finger. I wanted him to be the caregiver, macho and strong, yet gentle in how he looked at me. I wanted him to love my girlishness more than his own.

For others who know a relative who struggles with revealing their gender or sexual orientation, I beg you to take the uncomfortable, awkward steps to ask those seemingly impossible questions. Are you gay? Are you transgender? What can I do to help you?

If my father had not hurt me, Mom, and Peter so deeply, I might have learned the way to freedom. Accepting who Dad was would not have erased her legacy of hurt, but it would have liberated each of us from the falsehood of her hiding, pretending, and not being able to honor her truth.

This is what happened instead.

~ ~ ~

The next time I saw Dad was the last. With my holiday birthday upon us, we drove with Nia to Millie's recently acquired condominium in Quincy. The Boston suburb was silent except for the occasional sound of windshield scraping and snowplows pushing mounds of snow from the virtually empty streets.

We arrived early, sitting in the idling car to relish the heat and let Nia sleep for a few extra minutes. Watching the refracted sunlight shine on the icicles formed on the rain gutter outside Millie's front door, I considered leaving.

Visits with my father required that I camouflage memories and ignore his changed appearance. It was my vanity and fear that stopped me from analyzing Dad's feminine transformation. I could not bear another scar. I did not understand, and it was easier to avoid the truth than to open the conversation. The mark of Dad's dysfunction felt as visible to me as Harry Potter's lightning bolt, a disgrace that marked me as less, lower, cursed. So, I tossed my father's gender issues into the closet.

Dad answered the door, smiling. I noticed the same shine on his lips that he wore to Nia's birthday, along with a faint penciled brow, shoulder-length hair, and what looked like the start of breasts. Doug saw it, too, but gracefully allowed me to ignore it as I clung to what my childhood soul craved—a Daddy.

"Get in here. We don't want to let the cold in," Dad ordered.

I shivered at his commanding tone. Side hugs and cheek kisses commenced. Nia stretched, instantly enamored by the white lights on the green Christmas tree and the wrapped gifts beneath it.

Dad spoke in his usual flat, bragging tone. "Millie and I are heading to Europe again next month."

"Great, Dad, that'll be fun."

"Oh, we went to Davio's Steakhouse last week. Excellent service, spotless. You gotta try it."

"Dad, that's one of the most expensive restaurants in Boston. We can't go there."

"Maybe for Valentine's. I want to take you and Doug out with Millie."

The idea of spending Valentine's Day with my father, whose appearance had turned pink and whose demeanor remained black, hurt my stomach in the exact spot where my childhood ulcer burned. "We'll see, I might be going to Doug's family in Buffalo."

"Oh, you have to see the hutch I ordered in Thailand. It arrived last week and perks up my dining room."

"Our dining room," I mumbled, recalling Peter's unconscious body on the floor near the baseboard heater. Painful memories long suppressed swam up through the synapses; black and white photos bled crimson.

"Huh?" Dad looked confused.

"Nothing. Sounds nice."

Millie worked in the kitchen, opening and closing the oven to retrieve a roast. "Joe, it's close to done. Could you drain the carrots?"

"Sure. Don't let Nia touch the presents. I want pictures," he ordered, pointing at Nia with an authority that made my mom nerves sizzle.

Once he left the room, I looked at Doug. "I don't know if I can do this."

"You can. We won't stay long after dinner. Weather is rough anyway."

Nia sat on the beige carpet playing with her wooden pizza and placing painted pepperoni and mushrooms on the pie-shaped slices. She offered a piece to Doug, who pretended to gobble it down.

226

Dinner was awkward and cold. Nia rolled the boiled mini carrots across the oak table while seated in the booster we brought with us. "That's for eating, not for playing," Dad said, lifting a carrot to her mouth.

Instinctively grabbing the steak knife, I lowered it to my lap. Nia spit the carrot out, and I squeezed the handle tight, feeling the grain of the wood against the palm of my hand.

He put another carrot to her lips and pushed it in. Nia laughed, thinking it was a game, and spit the carrot onto the floor.

"You gotta eat," Dad said, bending to pick up the carrot and place it on his plate. A piece of the roast Doug had carved into tiny chewable bits was next.

"No, Dad. She doesn't," I exclaimed, sounding louder and angrier than I intended.

Doug grabbed my knee to quiet me.

"She ate before we came. It's okay if she doesn't want to."

My father looked at me, deciding whether to continue to force-feed my daughter. I spotted the familiar flash of anger in his eyes. Staring, I tapped the steak knife on my knee, silently daring him to continue.

Doug piped in, interrupting the battle, "Millie, potatoes are great. What's in them?"

"Oh, I made them," Dad's ego lit, deflecting his attention. "It's a recipe I got when I was in Germany."

Doug took the knife from me, casually placing it back on the napkin.

We finished the meal, listening to Dad and Millie talk about their travels.

While I helped remove the dishes, I let Nia explore the living room. She toddled about, playing with her toys and Doug, who repeated two words, that, for some reason, Nia thought hysterical.

"Oprah," he said, and giggling commenced.

"Oklahoma," he said. She laughed harder, falling to her knees near the presents.

Immediately enamored by the wrapping, she took a gift from the pile. Doug let her hold the present. "Wait for Grandpa, okay?"

Nia tilted her head, considering, then tore the corner of the silver wrap.

"I said she had to wait," my father's voice boomed through the condo.

"She is," Doug answered. "Just curious."

"We're not opening anything until Vicki-lynn opens her birthday present."

"It's okay, Dad," I answered, drying my hands on the towel I had carried into the living room. "I don't care if she opens it."

"Well, I do. Your birthday first."

"Fine. Whatever." I walked to Nia, taking the gift from her. "In a few minutes, honey." I lifted her to my hip. "You can help Mommy dry dishes."

She eyed the gift as I put it back under the tree, "I do dishes with Mommy."

"Yes, you do the dishes with me." I gave Doug a look of desperation.

Doug shrugged his shoulders. It was always the same with Dad. Free will be damned. It was his way or the highway. We followed the opening of presents with cake and numbing small talk. Nia played with the wrapping paper, tossing it back and forth to Doug, who sat with her on the floor near the Christmas tree.

Millie offered coffee, and we declined. "I think she's getting sleepy. We better get going." I looked at Doug, who nodded.

"So soon, we hardly got any time with her," Dad looked genuinely disappointed.

"Yeah, well, it's a long ride, and Santa comes early."

Millie helped us pack up Nia's gift in a Filene's shopping bag. "Thank you for dinner," I said.

"You know your father wants to see more of Nia. He's always showing off her photos."

"That's sweet. We both work, and you know how being a Mom is."

"He thinks you avoid him because your mother is so close now."

The sting and absurdity of the comment caught me off guard. "Uh, Mom has nothing to do with it. We're just busy. That's all."

I grabbed the bag and headed back to the living room, where Doug was packed and had already put Nia in her plaid-hooded coat.

Dad was taking photos, and I scooped Nia up mid-shot. "Well, heading out. Bye, Dad. Thank you for all the stuff," I said, pecking his cheek. It was the closest I had gotten to him all night, and I realized he smelled of gardenia.

"Okay, okay. Such a rush. Call as soon as you get home so we know you made it."

"Will do," I agreed as Doug shook Dad's hand awkwardly. Dad patted his shoulder, and we were off into the frigid air, a welcome awakening from the discomforting performance we'd enacted—pretending he was safe and caring, pretending he was male, pretending he had never drowned a moaning cat, and that I never tried to kill him.

32 The Towers

Three days after the Twin Towers fell and the world plummeted into before and after 9-11, Doug and I lay in bed watching television. Photos of the devastation flashed across the screen. The images pulled me back to a day thirty years prior when Mom had taken Peter and me to the World Trade Center construction site.

"Once we finish, they'll be the tallest buildings in America," my father had boasted.

I glanced down at my shiny patent leather shoes, which I had insisted on wearing despite Mom's warning that they'd get dirty. A coating of dust dulled their reflective surface. Looking up next, I asked my father, "Will you climb to heaven?"

"Yeah. Or I'll get fired, and you won't get no dinner tonight," he chuckled.

"Mommy," I tugged at her coat, "I don't care if we don't get dinner. Daddy can go to heaven."

The newscaster's lens focused on a survivor covered head to toe in dust. The woman walked through thick gray ash in the aftermath of the collapse, wearing a confused mask of despair, confusion, and need.

I dreamed of Dad that night and for several nights after. In those dreams, he tumbled from the buildings. Young and proud, he wore the same hard hat from the day I would have sent him to heaven.

On September 12, 2001, I called friends and family in New York. It seemed that all humankind reached out to reconnect that day after, except for my father. He never called, and my phone number had not changed since we last saw him. I worked in Needham, traveling out of Logan Airport for work. Every member of my family expressed their concern except Dad. It was the final betrayal of his fatherhood.

What I did not know was that while I was judging him as inept and absent, he was busy erasing the man I knew.

Since my father's death, I have learned that the process of becoming a woman does not begin or end with gender reassignment surgery. During that tumultuous year, Dad took significant steps toward becoming a woman. I learned of the increased cross-dressing in off-handed observations passed like a game of telephone from my mother, and her version came from stories shared by Aunt Shelley and Uncle Ronnie.

~ ~ ~

It was a frigid day in 2001 when Mom tickled the knowledge I had tucked away since my college homecoming sixteen years prior. Divorced for the second time, she had moved from Florida to Massachusetts to babysit Nia while Doug and I worked.

Hurrying around the back corner of the three-story house where Mom rented a basement apartment, a breeze swept in from the busy Atlantic, jostling the knit cap from my head. Mom's apartment welcomed with thick heat and a smell of chicken soup and Jean Nate.

Avoiding the piano mat that played music if you stepped on the vinyl keys, I grabbed Nia's coat. "Hey, Mom," I greeted, attempting to zip my daughter's fidgety frame into the cumbersome garment. Mom tossed toys from the floor to the closet. Nia wiggled away, crying, "Ganny."

I sat, happy for a break from the rushed deadlines of the day. Mom joined me on the couch. Nia stopped picking up toys once she got to the little people school bus. She ordered the round people to school, placing them in their respective seats.

"Joe visited the Silber's last week. In full dress."

"What? Like my wedding? A tuxedo in a sea of sports coats?" I laughed.

"No. Women's clothes. He wore a woman's pantsuit."

"Why?" I asked the simple question, unaware that the issue would become a lifelong quest for understanding.

"I guess he thinks he's a woman. Shelley said it's not pretty."

"Mom, I don't want to talk about him." Gone were the years of rushing forward as Dad smashed Mom. Like a battered turntable, my mind skipped over scratchy, damaged parts.

"I know, I know. But come on. Can you imagine him as a woman?" Mom laughed.

"No, and I don't want to." I grew irritated. "Time to go, Nia. Let's get your coat."

Nia dragged her coat along the carpet with one sleeve on and one off. As soon as she was close enough, I grabbed her, squeezing protectively.

"Too tight, Mommy," she whined.

"I know, baby." Her green eyes looked confused. "How much does Mommy love you?"

"Utterfly kisses."

"That's right. More than all the butterfly kisses."

Again, I pushed my father's truth from my mind. Neither appalled nor intrigued, Dad had finally become an abstract thought, fleeting, anesthetized. His power to hurt me had waned, and I refused to give him that power back.

He floated there, ignored and out of reach until the letter arrived four years later.

33 Glamor

In 1921, advertising executive Fred R. Barnard ran a magazine ad to promote the use of advertising on streetcars. It read, "One Look Is Worth a Thousand Words." Translated today as "A picture is worth a thousand words," the saying perfectly expresses this day.

I could not unsee it nor reasonably pretend that my father's gender was male. Still, I tried. Self-salvation, discomfort, hate, and a lack of understanding made me ill-equipped to truly see what I already knew. It was my turn to hide.

~ ~ ~

On a sun-soaked Monday in 2005, I sat in my home office sorting bills into *pay now* and *pay later* piles. "Hey Doug," I called to my husband. "Would you mind bringing in the mail? Want to see if there's anything I missed."

"Sure." He entered the room, fresh from an after-work shower. "You smell good," I said without turning around. Standing behind me, he flipped through the junk mail, and I looked up when I heard him exhale. Wearing a frown, he held a small, personal-size envelope. "It's from Joe."

Staring at the envelope, addressed in my father's awkward scrawl, I recognized the PO Box on the return label. Dad had started using it the year my parents divorced. It was his attempt at becoming untraceable—a stealthy soldier in a world that was out to get him.

Doug put his hands on my shoulders to quell the emotional sandblasting that happened as soon as Dad entered my atmosphere. I held the nearly weightless envelope like an offering, my stomach bubbling with the thick, rancid bile of a childhood gone wrong.

I left Dad behind after we moved to Savannah, Georgia, abandoning him for sanity, a chance at being a working family, and breathing room. I left behind the complications, wounds, and confusion his life represented to start fresh.

"How did he get our address?"

"No idea; what's it been? Four years?" Doug asked.

"Yeah, about that." I placed the envelope on my desk, a bright white contrast to the yellowed pages of *Jane Eyre* I'd pasted on the surface months before. "I don't want to go there. Can't he take a hint?"

"You know you have to open it." Doug squeezed my shoulders, attempting to lessen the tension. "The curiosity will drive you crazy. Just do it. You don't have to respond."

Shaking my head, I retrieved the bright blue opener from my pen cup. Slicing the pointy edge through the unwanted communication, I found another envelope inside, folded into three-quarters and blank. Inside the second envelope was a wallet-sized photograph.

Alien, yet familiar, it was a photo of my father. She was a woman.

Against a black studio background, she raised her chin, looking to the left. The red sheath, wrapped around her large frame like a strapless evening gown, revealed tan lines from her watch and typical short-sleeve attire. Her grayish-white hair puffed out at the back, leaving her large, Germanic forehead exposed. Thin eyebrows, lipstick, and expertly applied rouge completed her grim look.

Dad wore a face full of foundation and rouge. The glossy coverage of her pursed lips did not hide her former masculinity. The usual tension made her jaw look severe and dangerous. She wore her thin, gray hair parted to the side in loose waves. It fell over her ears, not quite reaching her broad slumping shoulders and cleavage. Her arms were crossed. She wore two silver rings, one on the finger where her wedding band had once promised a lifetime of honor.

I wondered for a moment why she chose this photo to send when the photographer must have taken several. The blank stare of her lined blue eyes and tight lips spoke of pain, not the relief one might expect. Her chest, sinewy above the makeshift red garment, was full below. My father had breasts.

"Holy mackerel." Doug's hands went limp on my shoulders.

"Oh, my God." I stood, my fight-or-flight instinct setting in. I wanted to run to the closet, crouch in the dark, and disappear.

My hands quaked, and the small photo with its immense complications fell to the carpeted floor, flipping once before landing face down.

"Put it away. Please take it. I can't. I just can't."

Brushing away the unfinished appearance of my father in transition was impossible. The gender-confusing image came to me in dreams as a teasing shuffle of playing cards. With each flip of the deck, a fresh picture emerged.

Dad with the hammer, dungarees bloodied from the self-mutilation that earned him an early retirement.

Dad in an evening gown dancing with a German grandmother and laughing.

Dad in our backyard, legs soaked, and eyes glazed over in rapture over the final howl of the drowned calico.

Dad in face makeup, melting like Batman's Joker, laughing, and applying layer upon layer of lipstick.

With Dad's secret exposed, it became my turn to hide.

34 Call me Jo

Like the bruise of a crocus on winter's pale complexion, my father ceased hiding sometime around 2005. Joseph became Joann. The moniker of her metamorphosis was a syllabic convenience. No need to alter the phone listing or monogrammed towels that hung threadbare in the basement washroom, an addition Dad built the year before she rented our childhood bedrooms to boarders.

The surgery did not assign Dad's gender. Transgender people know their gender long before a single snip, tuck, or stitch. They suffer with it, living in bodies they know to be a mistake. So, surgery was not necessary for my father to become a woman. However, she underwent full-gender reassignment surgery, including a vaginoplasty. She had makeup tattooed, her breasts enhanced, hormone therapy, and she lived wholly as a woman from the age of seventy until her death.

The last time I spoke to Dad, she was a woman I could no easier accept than the man. Our emotional conversation in 2010 slashed and swayed like all aspects of our father-daughter relationship. Tumult defined us and became our fitting goodbye.

~ ~ ~

I was drying dishes when the phone rang. Wiping the sudsy residue from my hands, I balanced the phone on my chin, "Hello."

The voice at the other end was unmistakable and jarring. A broad clearing of the throat preceded words, "I, this is your father."

An awkward silence crackled on the line. I held the phone at arm's length, a vile intruder into the normalcy I'd created during the five years since the transformed Jo photo arrived in the mail.

"Yes, Dad." I moved down the hall to my pondering place, the purple walls of my office a mellowing welcome for a conversation drenched in red memories.

"I've been looking for you. Hired an investigator to confirm your address." Jo cleared her throat again, obviously nervous.

The desk chair squealed as I settled in, looking for comfort. "I got the photo, so you had the address."

It was Dad's turn to be silent. I watched as twenty seconds ticked away on my desk's whimsical Hello Kitty clock.

Dad broke the silence, "I'm not flamboyant, you know."

"Okay." I touched my face instinctively, my father's words igniting the melting scars of childhood.

"I wanted to talk to you, but you disappeared from Gloucester. Why didn't you tell me where you moved?" Dad sounded desperate and small.

"Because I didn't want my daughter to experience the same dysfunction Peter and I did." I sat up straight, expecting Jo to pounce.

"I'm her grandfather." Dad's voice was impossibly soft and vulnerable.

"Yes, and you were supposed to be my father. But you did a piss-poor job of it."

"I've changed. I mean, I'm different now," Jo whispered.

I chuckled insincerely, "Yes, I saw. That has nothing to do with me talking to you."

"If it's not my lifestyle, why didn't you tell me you moved? I couldn't even tell you that Millie died." Jo covered the mouthpiece of the phone, releasing a muffled moan.

"She was a good person," I said, thrown by Dad's uncharacteristic fragility. "I didn't stop talking to you because you're a woman, Dad."

"Then, why?"

"Because you were a horrible, abusive father. The things you did were not human, and I decided to cut off contact so Nia will never have to experience that."

"I'd never hurt her," he said, the timbre of her voice changing from broken to bold.

Freed by the usual brusqueness in my father's voice, I retorted, "Dad, I'm glad you found who you are. I am. I'm not interested in rekindling anything, not because of your gender, but because you hurt us, and I'm allowed to heal.

"That means stepping away from my abuser, from you. I wish you well. I mean, maybe that's why you were so mean. Maybe being frustrated fueled your anger. Whatever it was hurt me; I'm not going back there."

Dad's hand covered the receiver again to hide her weeping.

"I'm not the same," she managed between restricted sobs. "I have changed."

"I know you have, and you know what? I forgive you, but I can't forget. I just can't. I gotta go."

"I'm in Hilton Head."

"What? South Carolina?"

"Yeah." The line went silent as I comprehended the effort. Dad had traveled to a city an hour from my Savannah home. Now what? *She's too close.* I thought, not knowing how to respond. My breathing increased as the irrational fear of being trapped rose.

"Dad, I don't want to… see you."

It was my turn to tear up. Am I the hard one? She was hurting, but the girl in me could think of nothing more than my brother's battered face. I wanted the hurt to fester for her as it did in me. I wanted Dad to know the pain of rejection and the repercussions of loving someone who could not even like you back.

Throat clearing, "Are you there, Vicki-lynn?"

"Yes. I'm here. Where were you? All those years? Was it this? You wanted to be a woman so badly you beat Mom because she was one? Did you hurt Peter because he was a boy?"

"No. I... Your mother pushed my buttons."

"So, you naturally slammed her head in the oven and turned it on?" The venom of the past overtook me, and acid churned into a stomachache.

"I don't want to tawk about that crap. Can I see you? I dress normally. Nothing flamboyant."

My mind raced; what's normal? Was it the man in the plaid work shirt and big boots who loathed everyone? Was it normal for a father to hate being a hard-hitting guy but play the role so well that his own family feared him?

"You there?"

"Yeah. I don't care what you look like, Dad. You were a monster, and I'm glad you figured out why. Maybe you can have a good life now."

"I don't remember it like dat."

"Of course not," I whispered.

"What?"

"Nothing, I have to go. You should not have come all this way and should have called first."

"Can you send me a photo of Nia? I would like to see her again."

"Sure. I guess. Dad, I hope you find happiness now. I hope it all works the way you planned."

Jo's emotions spilled over, and she did not cover the receiver.

"Bye, Dad."

I hit the silver button on the phone to end the call. Laying my head on the desk, I released my disappointment in great sobs. I was disappointed in him, in her, in myself. Maybe I'm the monster. "Perhaps it's me," I wailed.

35 Accused

Anger was the original impetus for writing this book. Accused of abandoning my father, disinherited, and wallowing in the hurt of losing our childhood belongings—dumped as trash and sold at auction by a stranger who had befriended Dad for a few short years—I began writing to show her our truth. I wanted her to hurt as we had. My inner child wanted her to give me our things, make amends, and pay me the inheritance she received despite what my family had endured.

Today, the anger comes and goes as pen touches paper, but mostly I write to understand how a childhood that might have been so sweet became so twisted. I write to overcome and rejoice in the life I have now, in the lessons learned from dysfunction, and the love bestowed on my daughter as my husband and I raised her to adulthood.

Had I inherited the Medford house, I might have burned it down. That was the dream. Incinerate the place that scorched my heart. Or maybe I would have died of a broken heart while liquidating my father's life. I might have found more pain than healing had she not written us out of the will and forbade Peter and me from entering the house even after her death.

Today, as I complete this story of my life as her daughter, I write to heal and not to blame the woman named Grace who inherited all the stolen remnants of mine and my father's truth.

Grace. Ironic. Liberating.

~ ~ ~

Dad died on February 5, 2015, on the very spot where I had once planned to kill him.

I received the phone message three days before the funeral. I did not recognize the number that lit my caller ID.

"I'm looking for Jo Selbach's daughter. I need to talk to her about Jo. Please call me back."

Thinking my father must be ill and curious about why they would contact me, I called the number.

"Is this Jo's daughter?" a husky woman's voice asked.

"Yes."

"Jo's dead. The funeral is in three days."

"What?" I dropped the phone.

"I can't. Are you crying?, the stranger blurted. "You abandoned her, and she loved you. I can't."

The phone faded and crackled as the woman handed it to someone else. "Hi. This is Grace's daughter. She was close to your Dad, and she's upset. Well, the funeral will be a military burial."

I choked, almost laughing, and then crying again. My father, the draft dodger, was to have a military funeral. "How did it happen?" I asked.

"Fell on the ice, we think. A neighbor found her on the front stoop."

"The front stoop?" I caught my breath at the enormity of the location. The stoop. She died there, after all. My mind reeled; the musk and sweat of the Medford closet filled my nostrils. My shoulders caved forward as they had in the small space where I'd failed to shoot Dad. Fate had finally exhaled. I thought I would be happy. Instead, I found it difficult to breathe.

243

"Yes."

"Why'd your mother say I abandoned Dad? I didn't." The wound of her comment reverberated as my trigger finger tapped the phone. I was angry again, as mad as the moment I'd unsheathed his weapon. I swallowed hard, trying to stop shaking.

"Well, she tried to see you. Drove to South Carolina, and you refused. She was so broken up. She was a kind woman."

"Yeah, well, Joe was a horrible man. He was a monster." I shook my head, trying to filter her accusation into my truth. Guilt stepped aside to let fury in.

"Well, I don't want to get into all of that. My mother just thought you should know Jo died," the stranger said.

"Your mother thinks I abandoned Jo?" my toes curled upward in the polka dot socks I'd borrowed from my daughter. Electricity traveled up my spine, and my breathing accelerated. My father's evil doing bubbled acidic in my throat, "Well, you should tell her about the man I knew," I spit the words like venom.

"You tell her how my father drowned cats for fun while I watched and how he brushed my brother's teeth until he was covered in blood. Or maybe tell her about the man who bashed my mother's head and then had her committed to an insane asylum because she seemed out of it?

"That's who I abandoned. I escaped the devil. Your mother may have known a kind woman, but my father was a monster, and he ruined us. He ruined me. You tell her that." I did not recognize the sounds from my mouth as the tremor took hold. It was the kind of broken wailing that any number of tears could not fix. Dad was dead, and I was accused by strangers who had never sopped up an ounce of the blood Dad spilled.

"I'm sorry. I don't know what to say. I can give you the number of the funeral home if you want." She answered in a placating tone that hinted at my being delusional, as if I could not be talking about Joann.

"Okay," I squawked, unable to catch my breath as I scribbled the number on the back of an envelope.

"Also, you might want to call Jo's lawyer."

"Oh, yes." I wrote down the name as the music entered to accompany a spin of thoughts. *You're the end of the rainbow, Daddy's Little Girl* filled my head. I was dancing with him, his sturdy shoulder smooth under the black tux jacket. The dance surfaced, a practiced refuge to help me believe in something good. But there was no redemption. I wanted to pummel the accusers with words I'd learned from my father. The man turned woman. The lost man. The man who raged for the woman's soul she buried.

"Where are you right now?" I asked.

"At the house."

"Medford? In my house?" They were in the kitchen of my youth, a place where mothers held together flaps of skin to stop the hemorrhaging. Blinded to the family of ghosts still waiting to escape the putrid bowels of the hellish house, they stood in the brown, lobster-boiling kitchen, accusing me of abandonment.

"Yes, your father's house," she corrected as if I needed reminding. As if I might have forgotten how she took it from us and gloated. As if I could forget living in apartment after dingy apartment while she renovated the blood-veined timbers of our home. "We have a lot of cleaning and sorting to do. Your father was quite the hoarder."

"I don't think so." I shook my head to escape the memories of the room these strangers now occupied, "Jo used to beat my mother if she left dishes in the sink. A hoarder, ha."

"Well, we could barely get through all the stuff from the front door to the kitchen."

"Like, real hoarding?" I asked, dumbfounded, picturing the pristine hallway, a clear shot to the door from the killing closet.

"Yeah, there's trash that looks like it has been here a year."

I pictured Dad standing in the kitchen, once spotless for hurt sake. "I don't believe it."

"Well, I should go," the stranger said. "We have a lot to do."

"Okay." I wiped the slick wetness that covered my cheeks, "Thank you for calling to tell me about him; I mean her. Sorry I screamed at you, goodbye."

I still wonder what wrangled Jo from the house that blizzardy day. I picture her pulling on a thick coat, likely hung on the railing that led up the stairs to the attic and tucking a scarf deep into the chest buttons. I wonder if the constant chill of old age made her turn up the once-locked thermostat meant to keep tenants of our childhood rooms from inflating the utility bill.

As during my childhood, I know she tugged at the inner door a good minute before the ice loosed enough for her to open it. Tapping on the storm window that replaced the screen every winter, she would have waited for the icy exterior to crack and fall away to the stoop below. The sound of the cracking ice likely matched the creak of her seventy-nine-year-old bones lifting from the living room chair. The less she moved, the less she hurt, so she sat, day and night, with and without. It was a loneliness that even becoming her most authentic self could not fill.

Did she think of our youthful, expectant faces, anxious to enter the home we had watched workers pull from the dust? Did she recall, with anything but hatred, my mother lingering behind, holding Peter's hand, or the backhanded smack that provoked the tear that ran down my brother's cheek?

Perhaps she stood, pondering the ghostly memories for too long. Maybe her heart's final excruciating burst came at the instant as she turned to close the screen against a fierce wind that came from and went nowhere and everywhere simultaneously.

Whether it was quick or slow, I know the slippery stoop exhaled that day, an audible gasp laced with the screams of the untold number of tears shed upon it. Under its shudder, her fur-lined boot slipped, the other sliding like mustard down a sloppy eater's chin.

Did she reach for the screen handle, the one I used as a target in the hot months when I aimed the shotgun at it? If so, like me, she missed her life-saving opportunity.

The hard landing of her cheek on the cement step stilled the screaming of old joints and a limbic system overwrought by years of anger and hiding. Did she weep into the melting ice pellets as the dying game began?

I do not believe there can be solace in death for the wicked. As my father Jo twisted, she must have faced the stolen cobblestones of the walkway, her words crashing through the fog of fading life. "You'll weed it until I say you're done, you lazy idiots."

I hope the bruised faces of my mother, first wife Penny, biological son Tommy, Peter, and I mocked her then as silent, weeping reminders of wasted efforts and immoral behavior. Honestly, I think her last thought would have bent away from empathy, passing the culpability as she—when he—so frequently did. She would have thought we should have listened, that the turmoil of our childhood was our creation.

Snow began to fall then, coating the blush of her cold cheeks with a sparkle she spent a lifetime trying to uncover.

I cannot know which way her neck aligned her final stare, but I hope she saw the speck of green in her precious cobbles. I am sure that a lone strand of vegetation grew under the fresh powder that moved farther and farther from her view, nestled in the dirt crevice.

As she lifted away, the cold was replaced by a warming sensation that would have moved in and out like a heartbeat. I hope that weedy survivor appeared immense, spreading despite her distance from it, blossoming with wispy tendrils and black buds. As the buds opened, I hope the slow-motion falling away of himself freed her to feel the depth of her female form for the first time.

I pray that harsh accusations and angry tirades went along with severed male parts to a place far below weedy roots and that she lifted, weightless, above the roof of the aging house, past the acre of woods where playtime tortured and cats lay crucified. I hope the maintained female became real, soft, and as fluid as a gossamer wedding gown. A flower of white surrounded by the essence of the black buds, opening to garden rose proportions. I hope she could finally see me and all the ways I loved, wanted, needed, and loathed her.

The End - A Eulogy Deleted

At age 53, I returned to my childhood home, whose hallways and landscape I've walked endlessly in memory. I was in New York to visit a high school friend and asked her to drive me to the Medford house. In the midst of writing down the memories for this book, I needed to see if the powerful urges of childhood would resurface.

The current owner seemed confused when I knocked on her door to ask permission. She agreed to allow me a peek into the backyard. The land was bulldozed bare and free from our hiding woodland and the aluminum patio that had witnessed unspoken horror. Gone were the redwood benches that had once crushed knees and the barrel where cats drowned mid-howl. Replaced by an in-ground pool in progress and an outdoor kitchen that made me feel unkempt and a little lost, the Selbach's nightmare landscape was re-invented.

Before leaving the house that clenched my fists for five decades, I looked for ghostly reflections of my father in the windows and found none. A breeze ruffled my hair, and I smiled as I looked at the newly impersonal facade of the haunting place. Stooping to collect a handful of clover from the lawn where I had picnicked with my brother, dreaming and plotting our escape, I watched the greenery wilt from the heat of my hand, and a rush of good fortune filled my heart. I was finally free.

I meant to end this book with the eulogy I wrote for my father just days after her death. Laced with hurt, anger, and devastation, the language of that missive sliced and deveined Jo's life into the tale of a good woman who was a horrid man.

Yet, my father's eulogy is not the end of this story. This morning, as I watched a hungry blue heron dive into the marshy green serenity of another Savannah dawn, I was enlightened by the goodness of my life.

In all the years before finding my biological family, I had fantasized that I had been born a twin. I felt connected to something I could not see nor name, and the twin fantasy remained just that. As I look around my beautiful home and celebrate my mothers, daughter, and husband, I know I have never been alone.

From the moment the brown-skinned nurse raised me in the air to expose my gender to my first mother, I was tethered to a being not of fleshy DNA but of spirit. Perhaps, a side effect of my mother's daily prayers and assurances as she spoke to me in the womb. She did so every day of her pregnancy, telling me about God and her hopes for my life. She told me I would be okay, even though we would not remain together.

The thing that sustained me through childhood and gave me the strength to lift weakling hands against my father was unnamable then. It did not need a name to protect me. My faith was not learned. It did not arrive at a white-bonneted baptism and was not birthed in a stained-glass church. Belief adhered to me before I arrived in a world that would test my fortitude a thousand times before my thirteenth birthday. It was formed in the hope of one mother for the fate of a child she would have to let go. The irony of that statement is not lost on me. For all of Christianity was born of the same concept.

The only time I felt detached from the belief I knew from infancy, was as I lifted the gun in my killing closet. Even then, in my most profound moment of fear and loathing, my spiritual twin stood up. The imagined movement of the crucifix forced my finger from the trigger, saving me from myself.

My killing closet had three walls and a gun. However, it is not a unique place. We, humans, are all prisoners of our killing closets at some time in our lives. Whether fear, turmoil, secrets, or emotion send us there, we are all vulnerable to its embrace.

My adoptive father lived in a killing closet of her own. She spent a lifetime trying to prove a masculinity that did not exist. Her abusive father defined her perception of maleness. Her killing closet was the physical entrapment of living in a body that did not match her gender knowledge and of society's impossible expectation that we all act, think, and live the same life.

My adoptive mother's killing closet was a dark enclosure built on fear. Fear of failing at marriage. Fear of losing the children she'd adopted. Fear of being unable to raise the other mother's children in a home with regular meals and warm clothing. My mother was trapped by a lack of education, her upbringing, and the raw, blood-streaked gore of domestic abuse.

My brother and I were drafted into our killing closets at birth. Our shared battlefield made us more than siblings. Bandages, broken promises, and our father's belt turned us into comrades, each dependent on the other for survival. Our common ground was pain, fear, and knowing the secret places—mental and physical—where we could hide.

No matter the depth or dimension of humanity's killing closets, my story proves that we are all born with everything we need to live a life of love and hope.

In our darkest hours, when scratchy situations seem impossible to solve, the door to the killing closet may feel stuck, immovable. However, locks will fail, and beasts be slayed if we open our hearts to possibility. With faith, all that binds us becomes memory, allowing the light of freedom to step in.

"Find Courage to Live the Life You Love"
(epitaph from my father's gravestone)

THE END

Afterward

I still fear Dad's ghostly specter more than four years after her death. Mostly at night, in those tentative moments when slumber teases and shadows pass. My common sense tells me it is just the streetlight out front, flickering on and off as the massive oak limb taps its glass. I shiver anyway; a ghostly visit and a chance to get the last word would be just her style.

I cover my eyes, my palms pressed tightly together. My cheek cools, resting once again on the wall of the killing closet. My stomach churns acidic, and I pray that she rests far from the living realm.

Forgiveness has begun to wrap its arms around her memory, but I have not forgotten the fear invoked in the time when she was he. I'm afraid I never will.

Neither Joann nor Joseph could be the father I needed. Joe was a self-centered, narcissistic, greedy, base, hot-headed, elitist, and racist human being. These tendencies were not born of a gender mismatch. However, I believe that hiding her true self fueled my father's rage.

Her mistakes painted my childhood tragic. Yet, I was also wrong to deny her that final meeting. It was wrong to steal our closure. I was not ready to see my father as a female. I'd spent a lifetime looking for a male role model, and I was unwilling to delete the hope that he might still emerge. Avoiding the female Jo kept the hope of my dream Daddy alive.

Fathers should not shatter the bones of their children, and fear should not define childhood. Perhaps Daddy was an evil man because she was never a man at all. The ill-fitting body she wore for more than sixty years tortured her and us. The grace and heavy toll of my pardon from physical abuse were solely due to my gender. Her physical sentence was my family's albatross. Denial is the devil's chief tormentor.

All that remains of my father now are wishes.

I wish she would have said, "I'm sorry."

I wish she didn't cry during our last conversation.

I wish that when we spoke, I had understood all I learned when just weeks after Dad's death, a famous athlete revealed that she was transgender, and gender became mainstream news.

I wish she could have been herself from the start.

I wish that "do not harm" were a rule for all parents and spouses.

I wish.

AUTHOR'S NOTE

This is a true story of my lived experiences. The events are portrayed to the best of my memory. While all the stories in this book are true, the conversations are not written to represent word-for-word transcripts. The dialogue is based on my recollections as well as descriptions from family members. I recreated events, locales, and conversations from decades-old memories. In some instances, the names of individuals and places have been changed to maintain their anonymity. I in no way represent any company, corporation, or brand, mentioned herein. The views expressed in this memoir are solely my own.

Bibliography

Copquin, Claudia Gryvatz. The Neighborhoods of Queens. Yale University Press, 2009.

Stryker, Susan, and Stephen Whittle, editors. The Transgender Studies Reader. 2006, doi:10.4324/9780203955055.

Hughes, C. J. "College Point, Queens/Living In -Attention, Shore Lovers." The New York Times, The New York Times, 21 Oct. 2011, www.nytimes.com/2011/10/23/realestate/college-point-queens-living-in-attention-shore-lovers.html.

"Ellis Island National Monument." Flora & Fauna | Denali | Oh, Ranger!, www.ohranger.com/ellis-island/immigration-journey.

Goldschein, Eric. "Amazing Pictures Of New York City In The Early 1900s." Business Insider, Business Insider, 15 Nov. 2011, www.businessinsider.com/history-of-new-york-famous-nyc-locations-in-pictures-2011-11/.

Acknowledgements and thanks to:

My mother Lillian for telling me the stories she spent a lifetime trying to forget.

My baby brother Peter for being and belonging in my life.

My husband, Douglas, who holds my hand when the nightmares come.

My daughter, Nia, who is my heart.

Aunt Rosalia Rosen (maternal), and Uncle Karl Baker (paternal) for filling in so many gaps and for encouraging me to finish this flesh-eating book.

Aunt Shelley and Uncle Ronnie Silber for sharing your memories, and for leaving me a legacy of love, pride, and protection.

First and forever friend Suzanne Silber, for being such an important part of my life and loving me unconditionally.

Gloria Shearin, my favorite neighbor and first reader.

Lynne Brophy, my friend and second reader.

Mark Mance and Bruce Westerlin of Northview Hotel Group for gifting me a room at Jekyll Island Club to complete this book.

My beautiful, honorable writing mentor and friend Rosemary Daniell (*Secrets of the Zona Rosa/Fatal Flowers*) and all the Zona Rosa Gods and Goddesses.

Grace Stevens (*No! Maybe? Yes! Living My Truth*) for sharing her truth and her time when I started this book.

Lady Gaga for the album *Joanne*, which was my constant companion while writing our story

About the Author

A nineties rock goddess, V.L. ditched journalism class after landing her first interview with the late great punk icon Joey Ramone. As a national music journalist, V.L.'s work appeared in *Metronome Magazine, CREEM*, and *The Boston Globe*.

Born in Brooklyn, New York, on Christmas Eve and adopted after seven months, V.L. was reborn in 1991 when she was reunited with her biological parents. She moved south to be closer to both.

V.L. lives in Savannah, Georgia, with her bass player husband and a precocious Pyrenees named Ozzy.

V.L. Brunskill is the author of the award-winning novel *Waving Backwards* (2015). Her stories and personal essays have appeared in numerous publications and blogs.

www.ingramcontent.com/pod-product-compliance
Lightning Source LLC
Chambersburg PA
CBHW021354090426
42742CB00009B/851